Duppy Conqueror

Also by Kwame Dawes

Kwame Dawes

Duppy Conqueror

NEW AND SELECTED POEMS

Edited by Matthew Shenoda

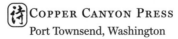 COPPER CANYON PRESS
Port Townsend, Washington

Cover art: Eugene Hyde, *Good Friday* (casualties series), 1978.
Collection: NGJ. Photo: Franz Marzouca

Copper Canyon Press is in residence at Fort Worden State Park in
Port Townsend, Washington, under the auspices of Centrum.
Centrum is a gathering place for artists and creative thinkers from
around the world, students of all ages and backgrounds, and audi-
ences seeking extraordinary cultural enrichment.

LIBRARY OF CONGRESS CATALOGING-IN-PUBLICATION DATA
Dawes, Kwame Senu Neville, 1962–
[Poems. Selections]
Duppy conqueror: new and selected poems / Kwame Dawes.
   pages;   cm.
ISBN 978-1-55659-423-6 (pbk.: alk. paper)
I. Title.
PR9265.9.D39D87 2013
811´.54 — dc23

                                                  2013005228

9 8 7 6 5 4 3 2 FIRST PRINTING

COPPER CANYON PRESS
Post Office Box 271
Port Townsend, Washington 98368
www.coppercanyonpress.org

For
Lorna
Sena, Kekeli, and Akua

For
Gwyneth, Kojo, Aba, Adjoa, and Kojovi

For
Mama the Great

And remembering
Neville

ACKNOWLEDGMENTS

All thanks to the editors of the following publications, in which these
poems — sometimes in different versions — originally appeared:

American Poetry Review: "Death: Baron Samedi," "To Tame the Savage
Beast," "Land," "Mama," and "Exorcism."

Narrative: "Avoiding the Spirits"

All thanks for the following publishers who first published the poems selected
for this anthology:

Peepal Tree Press for poems from *Progeny of Air, Prophets, Jacko Jacobus,
Requiem, Shook Foil, Impossible Flying, Hope's Hospice, Back of Mount
Peace,* and *Wheels*

Goose Lane Editions for poems from *Resisting the Anomie*

Ohio University Press for poems from *Midland*

Red Hen Press for poems from *Wisteria*

Parallel Press for poems from *Bruised Totems*

Stepping Stone Press for poems from *Brimming*

Akashic Books for poems from *Gomer's Song*

I offer much gratitude to Matthew Shenoda for his excellent editorial and
brilliant selection for this collection. I thank also the amazing Copper Canyon
team led by Michael Wiegers for making this book happen. Finally, I offer deep
gratitude for Jeremy Poynting of Peepal Tree Press for giving me a supportive
and constant home.

Contents

Bruised Totems *(2004)*

Brimming *(2006)*

Wisteria *(2006)*

Gomer's Song *(2007)*

Wheels (*2011*)

New Poems

Editor's Note

MATTHEW SHENODA

In approaching the work of Kwame Dawes for the first time, I was struck by the synergy I felt in his language, in his ability to cultivate all of my senses as a reader into a moment of reverie. His ability to transfix this reader into a single moment of being that disappears into the poem was a welcome reminder of why we all came to this art in the first place. Deft in the craft of persona, Dawes has the ability to transport the reader from the landscape of the earth to the landscape of the human spirit: this is his true virtuosity. His poems can switch so fluidly from poniards to ruminations, from social expressions to personal narratives. An exemplary model of the "reggae aesthetic" he has written about in his prose, Dawes's poetry embodies the political, spiritual, and sensual in a way few poets have mastered. His is a fully human poetry, a poetry engaged in a true sense of struggle. When I read the poetry of Kwame Dawes I am reminded of what the social theorist Eqbal Ahmed once argued: "Collectives of oppressed people discover themselves, their strengths and their humanity, through struggle. If you don't resist, you don't struggle, you don't discover it. You don't even discover your own humanity, much less that of others." His is a poetic praxis reminiscent of this struggle to discover one's humanity. It is at turns deeply comforting and unsettling. But one thing that I continue to return to, as a reader of Dawes's poetry, is the incredible sense of honesty found in his poems, and the almost ethereal sense that the lived experience of humanity, in all its glory and banality, is a sacred thing, a thing to be relished, no matter its condition.

Dawes's work has left me floored, not only by how prolific he has been in a relatively short time but also by the consistent quality of the work. Each of the sixteen collections sampled here is a brilliantly executed and thoughtfully conceived project. Dawes's reach and scope are wide and significant, from poems that explore the social conditions and realities of HIV and AIDS in Jamaica or African American history in the southern United States to poems that navigate the intimacies of mental illness or reminisce on childhood wonder or reflect on the influences of reggae music. The works included here are exceptional and wide-ranging, always laced with a tight sense of craft and intent, always full with music.

In speaking to fellow writers and readers, I found that although most have heard of Kwame Dawes, and indeed read some of his poetry, few knew the extent of his craft and body of work. The theme became clear: the few books published in the U.S. were known to American readers, and those who followed Caribbean literature were much more keenly aware of Dawes's immense bibliography. Those not as cued in to Caribbean literature were significantly less aware of his prolific accomplishments. Although all his books are written and published in English, most have been published in the U.K. This realization became another example to me of the gulf that is the Atlantic; even when language is not a barrier, we still seem to move within our own national and regional circles. What troubles me is a lingering parochialism here that is not in step with a global reality. Dawes has been a significant figure in American letters, having lived in the U.S. and participated vigorously in the shaping of its literary ethos for two decades. It became apparent to me that it was time Dawes's work got the attention it deserves, and if readers in the U.S. weren't going to go to the books published in the U.K., it was time we bring that work to readers in the U.S.

The new and selected works found here follow a timeline from his first published collection, *Progeny of Air,* to his significant body of new poems, a long meditation on the essential works of August Wilson, the great African American playwright. Each of the sections found in *Duppy Conqueror* samples from Dawes's best work, showing the seemingly unending arch and variances of a poet intent on finding his mastery and making a significant impact on contemporary global poetry. His is a unique position: born in Ghana, raised in Jamaica, partly educated in Canada, and living now in the U.S. with strong ties to the U.K., Dawes embodies a truly internationalist, African diasporic position. He is a leader of a new generation of Caribbean voices that, taking their cue from reggae music, are at once deeply rooted and yet wholly comfortable being "outernational."

Finally, the title *Duppy Conqueror* is borrowed from the Bob Marley track of the same name and was chosen as a kind of moniker that embodies Dawes's poetic aesthetic. In Jamaican culture, a duppy is a malevolent spirit often working toward a harmful outcome: a distractor of humanity, a spirit whose aim it is to derail the conscious struggle of people fighting for a just and right world. Each of us has our moments of embodying the duppy, of becoming "bull-bucka," and it becomes incumbent upon those interested in cultivating a reverence for the world around us to fight against this embodiment. It is an age-old story, really, and one that Kwame Dawes breathes new life into. As you read through Dawes's work, you become keenly aware of his ability to grapple with the duppy, both external and internal, and I edited this book in that spirit so as to honor the struggle that poets from various traditions have wrestled with for centuries. Dawes is a poet in that tradition, a poet who wishes to use his art not simply as a means of personal expression but as a way to shape our perception of, contextualization of, and conception of the world. Dawes is a poet unflinching in his ability to say what he means and to stand firm in his own humanity. His is an upright poetry, a poetry that is neither stringent nor irresolute. He is a poet who wishes to use his art to struggle against the afflictions that each of us must grapple with, that often we wish to ignore. His is an essential voice for our times, one that has not lost its sense of wonder or its understanding of the past. He seamlessly integrates the old ways with new realities and is unafraid to cast his net into unknown waters. His poetry is the antidote to the evil that too often surrounds us. As the Marley song goes, "So if you a bullbucka, let me tell you this—I'm a duppy conqueror." Dawes's poetry is that duppy conqueror, and we are all made greater in our ability to revel in it.

Duppy Conqueror

Progeny of Air

1994

Change

So a big boy would tell a little boy:
"Here is ten cents, now get me
from the tuck shop

two patties, a coco bread, a sugar bun,
a toto, a slice of cheese, and a cream soda;
and make sure you bring back the change."

They always picked the boys with the wavy hair,
clear eyes, and money in their skins.
They always got back change.

Barnabas Collins

I

Collingbush the short Englishman
drives a low-bellied green sports car
that kicks up the gravel and dust

where he parks under the ficus berry tree.
Collingbush walks with a hop and step
in brown-stained white shorts,

his jockstrap bulging phallic
for the coy schoolmistresses
who watch us gambol to his command in the April sun.

Collingbush's harsh commands
ring across the parched playing fields,
the boys like rebellious slaves

naming him in whispered tones:
"Barnabas, ole vampire!"
One day, one blazing-red October day,

red with the bad weed and mad to hell, Tippa turn into Tacky
and attack him for knocking the ball too hard. Tippa slap him
across the head, then sit on his chest and chant:

"Barnabas! Barnabas! Barnabas Collins!"
And Barnabas, flaming red with shame, like every good colonial
is practiced at nursing a grudge.

And Tippa, the stroke master of the side,
spend the rest of the season on the bench in full whites
pricking dots in the green score book.

II

Collingbush may have a wife
white like him and tanned orange
living in a roach-infested bungalow

down in the green madness of the
teachers' compound, but we don't know this for sure:
some think he is gay.

Does he know how we laugh at him,
how we snicker when he gives us tips
on strokes to make, how we long

for the ball during those Old Boys' games
to send one short of a length and rising
to startle his poor blond head with blood?

Collingbush has one friend
who smiles broken teeth and spectacles
like Collingford and speaks the same patois-

colored cockney of expatriates;
who teaches the same physical disciplines;
football, track, discus-throwing, swimming, cricket,

hockey, and a bit of stiff upper lip
at Meadowbrook School where the field
hugs the mountainside, and rain

is always sudden and decisive at cricket matches.
Each season they meet
to compare scars and plan their escape,

Collingbush and this long-haired hippie type.
I am convinced that somewhere in cooler London
there is a niche for these two estranged souls.

I think I missed him a year after his departure —
sometime in sixth form; sitting in the Hall of Fame perched
precariously in wood and brittle cement on the top of the Simms Building.

They say he went to a private school in Mandeville where it was
cooler and more hospitable to his kind.
I think back, searching for something he taught me,

some treasure of wisdom, some clue to my stroke play,
but I find only his broken teeth and bobbing head
screaming out commands in the blazing sun

making history lessons so damned pertinent;
Old Barnabas Collins in the metallic green
sports car kicking up the gravel under the giant berry tree;

hoarding all the new balls from our hungry fingers
in his linseed-and-sweat-smelling minicar boot,
and Tippa pricking balls in the green score book.

Excursion to Port Royal

i am inside of
history. its
hungrier than i
thot

ISHMAEL REED

In the giddy house   the wind riots on the beach
we have had a lunch of flat moist sandwiches cooked
by the steaming bus engine   now alone
abandoned by the other boys   I stare across the roll of sea
there is no sign of the passing of time

no evidence of the decades of progress
only the scraggly grass   the Institute of Jamaica
tourist information plaque screwed tight
into the armory wall   here is the possibility of journey
from the quarterdeck I claim all I survey

on Admiral Nelson's quarterdeck the sea sand is black
shells glint white in the tick of waves
the water is moving   the horizon shifts   the morning's clean edge
smudges into stark sheets of white light   a thin line of cloud
moves   the wind toying with its tail

cannon crusted with centuries of rust   black sea sand   dirt points
Admiral Nelson surveys the royal port from his quarterdeck
goblet of gold rum swishing in his unsteady hands   the bitch is singing
from the wooden whorehouse there a blue Yorkshire chantey   her tongue
is heavy on the vowels   his dick is erect

here was Napoléon's nemesis too   long-haired bitch with a royal name
teasing the rum to flame in the sweet roast-fish air   singing Josephines
their tongues dancing   in the voice you smell their sex

Nelson searches the horizon for a ship's sail needling its way
across the fabric of green silk looking for war

the shore crunches   laps   folds   unfolds   ticks   gravels
its undertow back out to the seaweed bed   the last of the rum
warms sweetly in his pit   the voice sirens across the quad
and making his giddy way past the armory   combustible
as the itch in his pants   Nelson prays for the empire

Progeny of Air

The propellers undress the sea;
the pattern of foam like a broken zip
opening where the bow cuts the wave

and closing in its wake. The seals bark.
Gulls call and dive, then soar loaded with catch.
The smell of rotting salmon lingers over the Bay

of Fundy, like a mortuary's disinfected air;
fish farms litter the coastline;
metal islands cultivating with scientific

precision these gray-black, pink-fleshed fish.
In the old days, salmon would leap up the river to spawn,
journeying against the current. They are

travelers: when tucked too low searching for
undertows to rest upon, they often scrape
their bellies on the sharp adze and bleed.

Now watch them turn and turn
in the cages waiting for the feed of
colorized herring to spit from the silver

computer bins over the islands of sea farms,
and General, the hugest of the salmon,
has a square nose where a seal chewed

on a superfreeze winter night when
her blood panicked and almost froze.
Jean Pierre, the technician and sea-cage guard,

thinks they should roast the General in onions
and fresh seawater. It is hard to read mercy
in his stare and matter-of-factly way.

He wears layers, fisherman's uniform,
passed from generation to generation:
the plaid shirt, the stained yellow jacket,

the ripped olive-green boots, the black
slack trousers with holes, the whiskers
and eye of sparkle, as if salt-sea has crystallized

on his sharp cornea. He guides the boat in;
spills us out after our visit with a grunt and grin,
willing us to wet our sneakers at the water's

edge. The sun blazes through the chill.
The motor stutters, the sea parts, and
then zips shut and still.

Stunned by their own intake of poison,
the salmon turn belly-up on the surface;
then sucked up by the plastic pescalator,

they plop limp and gasping in the sunlight.
One by one the gloved technicians
press with their thumbs the underside of the fish—

spilling the eggs into tiny cups
destined for the hatchery, anesthetized eyes'
glazed shock on the steel deck.

They know the males from the females:
always keep them apart, never let seed touch egg,
never let the wind carry the smell of birthing

through the June air. Unburdened now the fish
are flung back in — they twitch, then tentative
as hungover denizens of nightmares, they swim

the old Sisyphean orbit of their tiny cosmos.
The fish try to spawn at night
but only fart bubbles and herring.

On the beach the rank saltiness of murdered salmon
is thick in the air. Brown seaweed sucks up the blood.
The beach is a construction site of huge cement blocks

that moor the sea-cages when tossed eighty feet down.
They sink into the muddy floor of the bay and stick.
There is no way out of this prison for the salmon,

they spin and spin in the alga-green netting,
perpetually caught in limbo, waiting for years before
being drawn up and slaughtered, steaked and stewed.

And in the morning's silence,
the sun is turning over for a last doze,
and silver startles the placid ocean.

Against the gray-green of Deer Island
a salmon leaps in a magical arc,
slaps the metal walkway in a bounce,

and then dives, cutting the chilled water on the other side.
Swimming, swimming is General (this is my fantasy)
with the square nose and skin gone pink with seal bites,

escaping from this wall of nets and weed.
General swims upriver alone,
leaping the current with her empty womb,

leaping, still instinct, still traveling
to the edge of Lake Utopia, where
after so many journeyings, after abandoning

this secure world of spawning and living
at the delicate hands of technicians,
after denying herself social security and

the predictability of a steady feeding
and the safety from predator seal and osprey;
after enacting the Sisyphean patterns of all fish,

here, in the shadow of the Connors sardine factory,
she spawns her progeny of air and dies.

Akwaba

for Sena

I

Brown snow lines the roadways.
The still, gray city of whispers

in the sunrise, inches into bloom.
I see your slick wet head

swaddled in a sheet of blood,
your mother breathing into the half-light.

Sena! Wailing across my heart!

II

Lorna stares at the television
not recording the flicker of lights

just willing love to flow slow
in warm streams of her milk

into your quick-suck mouth
locked on like a fish in passion.

III

Picture this my heart's solace:
forever, I will watch your eyes

blaze through my dim, lensless blur.
Forever, sweet Sena,

Gift from God Almighty
Akwaba, akwaba, akwaba.

Resisting the Anomie

1995

After "Acceptance"

> Then I read the monumental legend of her love
> And grasp her wrinkled hands.
>
> NEVILLE DAWES, "ACCEPTANCE"

I

You were a child there
from two
to introverted ten
crafting your dreams
from tattered books
teacher Dawes crammed
onto his shelves.
Your brother was a knight
and your sisters princesses
and you wrote verse
because you longed for friends.

Curled in the cool underpart
of the creaking house on the hill
you battled chickens for space to sketch
the worlds in your head.

II

We drove there together once,
you, proud of the recollections stirred,
endeared each sharp bend in the road
with names like Breadfruit Curve,
Star Apple Corner, and Tamarind Arch.
Your laughter was nervous nearing the house,
the child in you drumming a rhythm
on the sweat-slick steering wheel.

On the slack porch you pointed
through breadfruit leaves
to the fading line of sea and sky
where Cuba wavered
in the midday haze.

From there as child
you learned of otherness, worlds beyond the house
afloat in a sea of green.
From there your home became
a point from which to leap.

   III

I walk the overgrown paths
where fired with Arthurian legends
you galloped, mad-child
on a wild irreverent steed
dizzy in the patchwork
of sunlight through the branches.

The thought of you as child
is real as the trees towering.
And staring upward
I trace your steps
avoiding the trunks
by the pattern of leaves
in the sky.

The child overwhelms
my straight-back logic
and suddenly I am sprinting
beating hoofbeats against my chest
light blazing green on my face
my shouts echoed in the tree trunks.

IV

On the barbecue
dry brown pimento beans roast,
the ancient chair she sat in
is there where a rotting orange tree
leans and sheds brittle leaves.
The chair is light and fading
sucked dry by sun and salt wind.

I can see her bandannaed there
sharp calico against the hill's gray
her wrinkled hands outstretched, trembling
her eyes glowing.

V

Maybe your ghosts hover above the house at night,
but I came at daytime, so I am not sure, but teachers,
you taught me much in the lesson of your silent ways.

While here, I smell ink and the dust sneezed as chalk dust.
Your world was a noble one, you cloud of holy witnesses
who sought new worlds to replace the chain-link silences.

Daily Bible verses etched on your brow missionary zeal
and gave strength to your upright eyes. Now you hover above
this house that crumbles where the wood ticks termites.

Maybe, grand ones, your ghosts linger above the house,
meeting there, then together swoop down, one wind
lifting a tattered sheet's edge — now animated, now brilliant O

cooling with a breath the sheen of toil on some weary back,
shifting breadfruit leaves to a rustling as eyes turn upward
smiling at the cool, not at you, not knowing that ghosts are wind.

You return morose, having done your part of touching the living
    before dawn
and getting little thanks for it. You return to your tombs in which
    you were sheltered
from the swelter of sun and the tramping of my feet now in the
    gray and green.

VI

I praise the dream of Sturge Town
and the silent homecoming it was.

I praise the songs of the ghosts
sealed in my mind's chrysalis.

I praise the constant leaves
spinning in the pure air.

I praise the hands that birthed you
worn as they were

for they glowed
stained red with first blood

spilled into this navel-string soil
where for years

the ancient red-barked trees
have stood.

I praise these things
freed by her wrinkled hands.

House Arrest

North Africa, 1961,
dusty yellow light spills
through the old window
throwing a black crucifix
where your body is flung,
stretched tense on the bed.

In half-light
a pyramid looms over the desert.
And closer to home
the mosque shudders
with low murmur
of acolytes to Allah facing east.

You say amen.

Downstairs, in the bar, the skinny pianist
with scabs for knuckles
coaxes "Bitter Fruit" from the out-of-tune grand
tucked in the smoky corner
and you play with the ash
on the puddled counter,
sipping gin while watching
for the man with red eyes at your back
with the gun and the tattered Sam Browne
smoking hash cigarettes at the door.

You, poet,
think predictably of last words
in case you were to die now,
last memories in case they were to shoot
before someone was contacted.

Choo-choo laboring
to birth number three
whom I haven't named.
Kenke and hot fish
from Achimota, some jazz offerings with nuts
in the senior common room,
Accra's highlife
of bright red sunsets.

You travel beyond to childhood,
measuring accomplishments
but finding only images
to be mustered and arranged.

Cuba peeping green and gray
long on the steady horizon.
Hills dense with breadfruit leaves,
a donkey cart on Sturge Town bends,
a cricket ball sailing smooth and low
to fine-leg after a flick of the wrist,
some old molasses and white rum
thick in the nostrils of friends.

And home, where is home
while you wait to die?

You write letters now
to mothers, mine and yours,
and I can hear them smiling when they read
Come home, Neville, come home.

The flight from North Africa to Beijing
was smooth and uneventful.

How many miles have you traveled from home,
journeyman from the archipelago
flung in arcs of seed through the air?
Broadcast, you land and sprout
renaming home with memories still echoing
in the poems you eke out.

Straitjacket and All

And at home,
in these wasted paradises
after the invasion and the raising
of the flag and Cain,
after the ousting of one dictator
and the installing of another,
the carcasses will be gnawed white
by the growing multitude of mad ants
building edifices of glory in the sand
over the tombs of the kings and princes —
teetering castles of Babel
that turn to mud and grime
and white aborted seed
when it rains pinpoint drops
from seeded clouds.

The earth trembles where the ants
now sheltered from the crumble of the castles
clamor below the carpet of grass.
This is the dungle,
here they masquerade
they skank hopelessly
to the insanity of Lee Scratch's dissonance
where once there was possibility
in the rebellion of discord.

They are the ganja-dazed acolytes
reggae's bottom beat
roosting on the Belleview sonata.
The march to the surface is clamorous
barely finding martial order when the chant
of the Youth deconstructs
the chain of sameness and repetition.

Hip-hop permeates the bassline:
strings patched digitally into the mesh
wash the cut of the cross-stick
on the one-drop rim's edge.
And suddenly they are running
without moving, feet slip-sliding
backward: Sisyphean youths
sweat and grins glowing
on their strained faces.

Dreaming on My Music Box

Bobbing and heaving dream man
I sleep under Cliff's Hanger —

reggae dance nights of wet dreams
on auto-rub-a-dub from dusk to dawn —

clicking back and forth on my tiny tape machine,
and I dream a rude girl with big brown eyes

feet locked into the black sand
on tough Port Royal rock, waist going wild

with a round-tipped pirate saber
driven through her soft center

spitting salty sea juices
thick as living blood.

She births blue babies
their wild white eyes waking me

to sunrise crawling on my sheet
drying my dreams to stone

guilt weighing me down.

History Lesson at Eight a.m.

History class at eight a.m.
Who discover Jamaica, class?
Christopher Columbus
Tell me when?
Fourteen ninety-two
And where?

Discovery Bay
Discovery Bay

Twisting through Mount Diablo
Where Juan de Bolas was hiding
Musket, fife, and powder
Guerilla, revolutionary
I am traveling to Discovery Bay
Traveling to Discovery Bay

How many ships?
Three ships
What them name?
Niña
One
Pinta
Two
Santa Maria
Tell me where?

Discovery Bay
Discovery Bay

Twisting through Fern Gully
Arawak blood was shed here

Crack their brains with musket shot
History is buried here
I am traveling to Discovery Bay
Traveling to Discovery Bay

Who lived here first?
Arawak and Carib
What were the Arawak?
Peaceful flat-head people
What were the Caribs?
Cannibals
Cannibals?
Yes, cannibals!
Now tell me where?

Discovery Bay
Discovery Bay

Rush past Saint Ann's Bay
Marcus was preaching from the altar
See the slave auction inna Falmouth
Cane field wild with fire
I am traveling to Discovery Bay
Traveling to Discovery Bay

You teach me all kind of madness
From Hawkins to Drake to Pizarro
From Cortés to Penn to Venables
At eight a.m. each blessed day
No wonder I can't find Discovery Bay
Was looking for the gold
And all I see is blood
All I see is blood
All I see is blood

Prophets

1995

Chapter X

Hermit

I

In the filthy caves of Wareika, not Arawak bones
not hieroglyphs on the wall, just the Eritrean warriors,
heads too large, facing the Italian cavalry:

the blood of the white dead on the grass
in fading red; the golden brass of the Emperor's
mounted army; horses breathing fire.

This apocalyptic vision's set among the bones
of slaughtered goats, discarded garments,
and the stale smell of smoke and urine.

In the yard, a mist ascends from the chillum
bubbling, and Ras Pedro, now street derelict,
hermit, whose unshorn locks cake

for want of practicing ritual ablutions,
sucks in his daily dreams and revelations,
looking like the prophets of old gone mad.

The posses in hiding (most-wanted fugitives)
package pieces of pork each Sunday for a joke
and send a red-haired nigger orphan to Pedro

and his cracked drum. The dread accepts
the degenerate flesh — only, he says, to protect
another from partaking of its poison: "I shall

burn it on this holy mountain, as a fragrant
offering to Satan!" He does not touch the bloodied
newspaper. "Res' it over yonder in my shrine

to the shitty of Nineveh." He points to his latrine
where the groan of sluggish blue flies emanates.
Then at night, when the trouble of rapid digital

basslines climbs the craggy marl path to his cave
of bamboo and cardboard, he swallows the abomination,
stewed in onions and wild herb for cleansing,

peppered out with the Scotch bonnets growing
like red sentries around his encampment.
Belching, humble and penitent, he asks Jah

for mercy. The goats are all dead now, their horns
piled in the broken shack to be used for his
mounded grave — this according to his last will and

testament scrawled in thirty exercise books
and still growing. From the slopes of Wareika,
Pedro observes his vast domain — the circle of magic

lights, the stadium constructed by Babylon where
once he sheltered in its unused tunnels until
the Queen of whores came visiting, and the walls

were limed to glorious white, and the prophets
were slaughtered, exiled to the hills, or locked into
the bedlam of Belleview's knocking fans.

Pedro's drums are cracked now; the skins
have been stewed in curry and boiled;
he has eaten his gospel of truth.

II

Clarice, who was born with his seer's eye,
has flown over the foothills and planted her
feet of news on the old beaten yard where as child

she mustered the chickens and sacrificial goats;
and at night serviced Pedro's lust and dreams.
Drawing back the curtain she saw Lot drunk and naked,

his black snake nodding on his thigh.
Having seen, she was taken.
Pedro prophesied her name in '58:

Clarice with eyes that penetrate
the sinew and bone; Clarice, with her mother's
skin and cheekbones, whose nimble fingers

construct fantastic designs from tattered fabric;
Clarice, the weaver of his nets; Clarice, waiting
there in the doorway for the weary drag of his

proud fisherman's body up the hill,
with sprat and snapper in his crocus bag
and the smell of sea in his beard;

Clarice, who spoke in strange tongues without prompting
on a night of drumming and revelations,
while the teenage would-be superstars,

climbing up from Channel One Studios with their
makeshift box-guitars and their heads full of songs
and fire, came to chant grounations with Pedro the teacher.

(Those who made it mention him in nostalgia
in their interviews, like one who died young,
lamenting their lost days of purity and righteousness

while they ride, bellies full, through New York and
L.A., sucking caviar, champagne, and custom-built
spliffs. Pedro is legend. That is all. Not even a smalls of gratitude.)

Back then, Clarice, the daughter in her righteous skirt,
would cook ital for the congregation of stoned
reggae denizens, playing her mother who, now

Miami-based, constructs a new past
in Fort Lauderdale, a past that excludes Pedro
and his slant-eye daughter.

Clarice saw her period motherless
and buried her wound in crocus sheets
until the first moon had passed.

Now, after all these years of absence,
after the secret departure one schoolday morning,
after the visit to the Government Office to declare

herself delinquent and a whore, after all these years,
Clarice returns in flight, her tongue now trimmed
to King James's metaphors, and she plants

a blessed kiss on his head. With no remorse
she promises to bury him well when he is ready.
She avoids the salvation message; his future is written,

prophesied and lived already; this interim
is redundant; nothing new will come,
marking time like this on the cloud of weed.

She carries a balm for his head and ministers it,
coughing at the dry smell of old sweat and sensi.
Found there in his nakedness again, this time he is

as potent as a discarded branch gathering dust.
In the hills, the guns echo where the posses
practice dodging Babylon's slings and arrows.

Pedro dreams, daughterless like this,
the chasm too wide; another life caught in the
bramble, another life bleating for attention;

but he is too old to try for another slaughtering,
another bloodying of the holy altar.
Clarice sees him beat his broken drum

again in the interim, the brief hiatus before flight,
his feathers drooping, tattered at the ends,
some broken at the quill: his wings, his

dull filthy wings. She sees his eyes: cataracts
consuming the light, no revelations on the cornea,
no premonition of safe landing on the plains

of Kilimanjaro, no Nile silver and blue
to barge down crowned in righteous glory,
no fledgling princesses to caress his wrinkled back,

no stool in the kraal with the shape of his buttocks
imprinted in the seat, no elders to meet him,
just this blurred spread of orange lights:

Kingston, the black of the sea, and the night.
Clarice takes his wrinkled face in her hands
and daubs the tears and caked matter from his eyes,

then brushes the gravel off his lips
with her own; he is not dead yet
this her father, broken prophet.

III

Clarice abandons this Hades,
this reaching for hope and not touching,
this her perpetual nightmare,

her reminder of where she has come from.
Waking in the silence of the Castleberry mansion
she bursts into tongues, praying, "Mercy, mercy!"

Chapter XVII

It Is the Cause (Belleview Ska)

> Love is Earth's mission
> despite the massed dead
>
> ANTHONY MCNEILL

I

The first visitation came riding the flapping
coattails of a ska syncopation, and the
rudies with their dawtas in miniskirts

and helmet heads smelling of the singe of the iron,
chopped scissor-slashes between their legs,
bowed, bobbed, grinned through the sweat,

eyes blazing like midnight riders in the Glass
Bucket Wine and Dinery to the blast
of Django's gunfire first, then the trombone calling

back across the black sand of the southern coast,
Yallahs, where the slaves buried the laid-out
body of Queenie, now traveling the miles

to familiar soil, Takoradi, Lomé, leaving behind
a dynasty of prophetesses, who now spray the rum
and shuffle in the dust yards around the pole.

The ghost with cauled eyes
and a green vision of Addis Ababa
lingering like sand in his soft eyelashes

is silent on the bandstand, watching
Africa in the dances of these partygoers,
here in Kingston's hip jazz clubs of the sixties.

He is eyeing like a dream the pelvic flirtations
of Anita, the rumba queen, whose hopes of
heaven in Batista's Cuba have blown up red

like revolution, and now she ekes a less glamorous
fame in the shabby ballrooms of the city,
waiting for New York to call, for Vegas, for Frisco Bay.

The horn man intoxicates his
vulnerable mind with her perfume.
"O prophet, how can you see through

this haze?" wails David over
the fetal remains of his misconceived
offspring, the ghost of the Hittite

walking the old balconies
where Bathsheba shed her skin
and threw fidelity to the wind.

And Joseph, sprinting in his Technicolor
dreamcoat with a voice sweet as a choirboy,
gropes in the corner for his tampered testicles,

and, wincing at the high laughter of Potiphar's wife
watching his frisky righteous butt vanish
behind the arras, says: "Don't do it, don't do it!"

"Don't do it!" says Elijah beneath the naked tree
in the wake of his lust for Jezebel, whose flesh
nourishes the dogs that shit her out into the fecal rivers.

But Don, the horn man, pulling his bell,
finding the distempered melody
in his puffed cheeks, his tongue

toying with the brass, tonguing the
patois into the ride of the ska,
the ride of the new jazz from Alpha

to the Omega of Thalbot's fertile soul,
what does he care about the cuckolded Panamanian
boxer, Anita's old custodian and pimp,

in this fire of their silent lust
burning up the Glass Bucket's dance floor,
making the prophet fall like that?

And when the Cosmic journeys after
the falling of his mind in Belleview's silent
dust, it is the murderer's gaze that leads,

as with fired missionary zeal, white shirt
tucked tidy, standing there with three
days' sweat and as many sleepless nights

in his eyes—he guides the traffic
in Cross Roads' crisscross of lanes with his finger,
a rotating compass making perfect circles.

In his head the blast of horns,
the impatient expletives are applause;
the rotten fruit, bouquets of roses.

Possessed like this, after near twenty years,
after the secret burial in the Catholic cemetery
with a weeping mother and priest and nun

who minister over this self-abused soul,
praying their penance for the last rites;
after the natty dreads recapture the tombstone

in Jah's name with rituals of incense and sensi;
after the cut of the kete in the midnight air;
after the gunshot and arrests; after all this,

the spirit of Don the horn man reinvents itself
in Thalbot, the prophet, who guides the Black Maria
to an empty alcove, and waits, arms outstretched, for the bangles.

II

Waving away the cobwebs,
he follows the path into the gloomy
belly of the shuddering van,

and carried away like Bedward
to the fluid calmness of injections,
the white walls and bed,

in his head the song again:
"You pray tonight, Anita?
It is the cause, it is the cause. Whore!"

III

The boys sprint in the interim,
riding the smoky jolly buses,
chanting, chanting. The traffic renews

its own insanity, and a generation abandoned
by its prophets and dreamers
searches for its old vomit,

while the horn man, blinded,
sees the machete dripping blood.
Anita's wounds, like Caesar's,

sing their arias:
the accusers at last finding
voice on her porcelain belly.

Chapter XXVIII

Flight

I

And when I die, I will fly. What promises you have for me?
Call it a bargain-basement faith, but I have to find
something what can fit my broad hip and match my

complexion. What you have for me? When I die
my pains will be no more; I will touch clouds
damp with next week's storms, over

the cedars and pines, above the smooth green
thighs of the Blue Mountains, and when I dip like a bucket,
the water from the rocks will be cool blue.

My watertight goatskin satchel will carry
smooth stones, cooling pebbles for under my tongue
when the harmattan dries the Atlantic

air waves. I will fly over Cuba
and say a prayer for Fidel (stroking my chin), for
despite the bad press, defecting daughters, et cetera, I dig

the man for his cynic's wit and mannish ways. Look the
boatload of criminals he liberate on Miami's
red, white, and oil-blue shore, and see how blood flow—

sangre de dios—in the palmetto beachhead when each defectee
prance the golden roads with scar-face badness,
dusting the green with coke like wedding rice.

Though hesitant, I will pit-stop over Babylon,
in some third-world barrio like South Carolina's low country
or them turtle-green islands where they preserve

the tongue of Africa, lodged in seed and stomach,
static magic swirling on Sycorax's fantastic Bermudes,
where black man Caliban still howls his panting heart.

Then it's east, for the cold bite hugging too tight
the Atlantic rocks. East it is, for this soulful flight,
looking, looking for soil to plant in — looking, sniffing.

East along the channels of air, warm Gabon air,
smelling the *akra*'s mellow smoothness, the sweet
kelewele, calling, calling, drawing me along the warm

currents. I'm flying east for the fleshpots
of Cairo, the Sphinx, the Pyramids — not home,
just legacies of gifts we have left, simple skeletons.

There on Cairo's streets, panoramas of faces
whip by like old statues of ancient times,
while the Black American intellectuals sip sweet coffee

in the cafés, retrieving their lost heritage in the colonizer's
tongue. Ah, the relics of our lost histories, the things
we have lost — seeking out a Black Atlantis so far, so far

from the conclave of huts and the circle of the griot's music
in the south, where green explodes in mountains
rising out of the brittle grit and dust of the Sahara.

Whitewashed memories are shored up in colorful texts
and clichés of a glorious race. Divided is Africa;
the Egyptians wince at the kente and dashiki.

Fly, I must, from this museum of broken dreams;
fly, I must, south to the antiphonal howls of the
Mahotella Queens, the magic of the Mokola daughters,

the flaring nostrils of the township shebeens,
speaking easy their histories in the firelight;
their eyes staring far like the Masai's gaze.

This is my dignity, this my familiar earth, this my arrival,
still damp with the dew of tomorrow's rain.
I alight without fanfare from the blue; the earth

reaches up its red fingers and sucks me, legs first,
deep into the blooming bottomland. This yank
tautens my neck like a kite rope, my head a dignity flag.

This is my dignity, constructed by so many journeys.
Why must I stay satisfied with rumors
of old women's proverbs and the *brujo*'s sharp

recognition of healing in each weed, bush, and turning
leaf? Return I must to that old shrine, now broken,
for those left behind forgot to feed the soil.

Shrine of my deepest fears, whose fingers reach
across the centuries and touch my eyes, my offspring
wrestling with the Holy Ghost found in the mountain chapel;

shrine of my deepest fears, split in my devotion
from the earth that beckons me with her smell of seed
to the new libation of blood shed for remission of sin;

shrine of my deepest fears, have you not heard that I wept
and felt the fingers on my cheek wiping, wiping;
that I have dreamed of another land, comely, home?

Shrine of my deepest fears, path to my distant time,
not that path which would find me back in Jericho,
or as nigger Simon on Golgotha staring at the black sky;

shrine of my deepest fears, what wind is blowing now
to meet my uneasy mind? I feel the travail in my bones.
What do you have to offer, dare I fall open before you?

Then, land I have heard about,
will you rise before my face from the spread
of desert and thick bush, Kilimanjaro

probing the cloud cover? Is this my
Eden, my heaven? Have you something better?
Have you a truth to plant me like a tree?

           II

Culture is flux. Flux is culture. Absolute spirit.
Is spirit absolutely true? Heart is not history. Heart of stone.
Heart is the fire caught-up within my bones.

Heart is prophecy frothing to the stomp and rattle
of the gospeler's Sunday. Heart is the word spoken
so deep in the stomach, so jealously protective of my soul.

Heart is my eye peering into our collective pasts
and, finding that ancient shrine in some broken hut,
drawing me. I arrive a stranger. I arrive dead. Sleep

never comes easy, for the trees of the mountain sanctuary
rustle their hymns, calling me back, calling me back.
Flux is culture. Culture is flux. We are changing inside.

III

The dashiki I wear is a flag.
Calls me dignified. The kente, a gift
from the Ghanaian attaché, my banner.

The sandals and the dust, my contact
with the earth. There is no burden of guilt
in my history; I will not share the blame for the callous

whip; the gospel of enslavement,
justified sardining of humanity
in our own juices, value packaged

and shipped with the blessing and guiding eye
of the all-seeing papal man; nor for the stolen gold;
the satchel of smallpox and rude disease;

the blood spilled; the betrayal and slaughter of Toussaint;
Sam Sharpe bleeding in the cane fields;
the dangling of Bogle; the black and white churches;

the rejected cornerstones falling, falling in the
black water of your hell; the silencing of my songs.
I will not be no beast of burden for you no more.

I reject twilight schizophrenia; illusions
of white Jesus with his red heart
enshrined in thorns, and his hippie

hair smoothly permed as he stands propped by
his Anglo disciples with thin, stiff upper lips;
I reject, too, the Academy of Regret;

your constant belief in the beauty and joy
of Colón's accidental landing; the perpetual admonition
to avoid the backward glance for your sake;

as if it were I facing the judgment
of salt and fire, as if I had left nothing
of beauty in the old village by the sea.

No, I will not deny the prophet with
wicked locks and a Trench Town bob
in his rhygin walk who says look back,

for that yoke is easy and the burden light,
and our legacy is more than the homelessness
of the sea — I have planted seed and it has sprouted

in this new soil, I have wailed to the hills
and my voice has returned dew soft
with clear melody and the harmony

of new trees, new brooks, new light;
the antiphonal prayers of old bones
calling me to take shelter in the green.

So there's nothing strange here;
nothing odd in my ancient garb
and the path of my metaphors.

You have, I know, heard it all before,
and more sweetly spoken, I am sure;
but I repeat the litany to clear the table

so we may start afresh. Now, clean as I am,
plealess; now that we know the lay of the land,
offer me what you have for me — go on. I am listening.

You see, I've always known this stuff —
this stuffing of history — to be
the baggage of your sterile sermons;

secretly concealed behind those curtains
while you down the best part of the wine
after we've just dipped and sipped small;

behind your Oxford tongue, acrobatic
around that clean sermon of bloodless salvation;
locked up in some closet, all this stuff

is sitting there, and if it wasn't for that smell,
that thick muggy smell seeping through,
I would never know you had all this stuff.

IV

I have come like this to see you point me
out in my cloth from Togoland and my
ragamuffin gait. Finger me now, I don't

give a damn who sees. I won't cause no
trouble. Tell the ushers to stay cool. I will smile
'cause I come to find a path — and this won't be

a path you make, it will be a path you may offer,
then I will decide and either walk the asphalt
or ride the cobalt sky on that chartered journey back.

See me sometime as your old black ancestor
before Peter at the door, proffering her
letter of recommendation to be relayed up

the ladder to God's desk or to his well-paid
letter writers: the risen popes, Paul, Newton, Augustine
of the burning groin. Like her, I come

like a comma to replace the closure
of your periods, screwing up the text
until the end is somewhere in the middle.

Now, tell me, what you have for me,
for this Sowetan gumboot dancer,
this Akan mother transported like a scroll,

discovered here where the bush still parts
for her footfall, slowly marching
from the sea inland to the sound of the drum?

What you have to offer me to break this miasma
of uncertain homes? What promises can speak above
the smell clamoring behind the curtains?

You see, the path you raise your left finger to
is a false path, o false prophet. This I have
seen. My morning songs lift me beyond

the chaos of your many and twisted roads.
Flying comes so natural to me these days
as I ride this sun-full, misty morning to Heartease.

          v

I am reluctant to leave it like this;
the tricks, the sin, the betrayals, as if this were all.
My journey has drawn me astray and, remiss,

I am turning to the old songs. Marley's call
from the darkness is pure light and hope
despite the countless dead by unbelief.

This song has wallowed in its grief
as if there were no music in the bright aftermornings,
no prayer caught in the mist's delicate sieve.

Now, rising up like a fisherman's weighted seine
to God, the tambourines celebrate the joy of faith rewarded,
the sickly child awakening after prayer,

sight returned to a warped cornea,
hope in a miracle of a child born intact.
How green is the island when it rains!

This song has lamented like a spoiled child,
yet how can I turn from these miracles
without tears of thanksgiving in my eye?

I write these poems with trepidation,
as if this tantrum might bring down the wrath
of the Almighty. But the prophets no longer groan

through the stinking city. Their feet skip on the mountains.
The cleansed are dancing on the hill's broken path.
Now, there is laughter and belief in mornings.

Jacko Jacobus

1996

A Way of Seeing

It all comes from this dark dirt,
memory as casual as a laborer.

Remembrances of ancestors
kept in trinkets, tiny remains

that would madden anthropologists
with their namelessness.

No records, just smells of stories
passing through most tenuous links,

trusting in the birthing of seed from seed;
this calabash bowl of Great-grand

Martha, born a slave's child;
this bundle of socks, unused

thick woolen things for the snow —
he died, Uncle Felix, before the ship

pushed off the Kingston wharf,
nosing for winter, for London.

He never used the socks, just
had them buried with him.

So, sometimes forgetting the panorama
these poems focus like a tunnel,

to a way of seeing time past,
a way of seeing the dead.

Emigrant

With nothing but a bag
pack with yam and bread,

a few coins in his pocket
to multiply into food,

Jacko board the ship for Charleston,
with not even a map to tell him where

this black liner heading,
just watching the way it leave a trail,

long and white in the soft waters,
and the way the mountains start to fade,

till nothing else was left but sea.
Jacko and the day grow dark.

Leaving behind love, leaving behind mother,
leaving behind a naked brother, red with anger,

leaving behind a father to bury himself,
a father weeping psalms of regret to God.

Find yuh Uncle Al, my brother,
and marry one of him pretty daughter dem,

den multiply yuhself, son,
till you is nothing but blood and water,

multiply yuhself, son,
so yuh inheritance might breed life.

Jacko meet a young hustler
with glitter in his eyes

talking 'bout how money easy
in the peach fields of North Carolina

and work easy for hardworking man,
and that was his only plan.

Now darting like a kite abandoned
to the wind, trying to forget that him have

a history, trying to forget there is
a place called yard, called house, called home,

when the dark embrace the ship
way out on the Caribbean Sea,

cut off, cut off so far from shore
Jacko toss the Bible overboard,

him hear it touch the water sof'.
The boat trundle on.

Trickster I

for Winston Rodney

Geriatric, wizened, ancient man

with a beard constantly damp from the flow of good and pleasant
nectar; our cedar of Lebanon,

evergreen griot, since forever chanting
fires down below, blowing up

like volcanoes, revolution;
hearing you now chanting,

isolated prophet on the beaches,
preacher preaching on the burning shore,

yes, Winston Rodney, you could never
forget your roots, such roots,

mellow like waves along the jumping
bassline — this big sound of primordial rhythm.

Yes, if we have a true prophet,
sallow and enigmatic with grandaddy charm,

like John the Baptist with his head full of lichens,
mouth full of locusts and wildest honey;

if ever there was a prophet to walk
these bloodred streets of Kingston,

to sing traveling, traveling, we still traveling —
despite the amassed dead and the fire,

we still traveling—it is you, reggae elderman,
spear flaming through the cankered landscapes:

in the steaming clubs of Halifax,
the kerosene jazz dens of Soweto,

the red-lit drug dens of Amsterdam,
the gritty damp of London's Soho.

We believe in the words of the prophet,
transported as we are by the regal one-drop

to a time when the seashells glinted
on the splendid Nile, blue and sparkling white.

Trickster II

for Lee "Scratch" Perry

I

A voice cried out in the wilderness.
We all came to hear the voice

in the Cockpit valleys, to hear
the man with a skull in his hands.

He was mad.
It was all quite obvious.

We listened but saw no revelations,
just a sweet madness of new rhythms.

Afterward, we drank mannish water,
ate curried goat, and slept peacefully.

II

Legend puts the Scratch man in trees,
comfortable in this lofty nest, where airwaves

have a clearer path to the sampling antennæ
of his dangerous, bright mind.

A few were baptized to the strange
syncopations of unsteady sycophants,

but all looked to see the boy
with a sweet falsetto grained with desert grit

singing the father's songs, just as
the Scratch man prophesied would happen.

III

There would be no wailing songs
without the madness of Scratch Perry;

none of the wild weirdness of *Kaya,*
none of the leap of images, enigmatic

mysteries like scripture; none of the miracle
of guitars twined each on each,

without this man, with his fired
brain and fingers of brilliant innovation

tweaking the nine-track sound board,
teasing out new ways to see heaven.

There would be nothing of the crucifixion,
no resurrection repeated each time another

reggae operator is born, again, again,
no revolution without this locust-eating prophet.

IV

All that is left is his bodiless head
chatting, chatting, tongue like a flapping bell,

tongue among the teeth. Salome too is dead,
but the head still creates this twisted

sound here on Switzerland's slopes.
Rastaman defies the chill and prophesies,

his head on a compact disc like a platter
spinning, spinning, spinning, new sounds.

Trickster III

This bassline is sticky like asphalt
and wet like molasses heated nice and hot,

and the bass drum booms my heart,
jumping me, jump-starting me

to find the path of this sluggish sound;
I follow the tap like a fly catching light

in its rainbow gossamer wings
on top of a big-ear elephant;

I follow the pluck of a mute lead-guitar string,
tacking, tacking out a tattoo to the bassline;

I let the syrup surround my legs
and my waist is moving without a cue,

without a clue of where we are going,
walking on the spot like this.

Coolly, deadly, roots sound on my back,
and I can conjure hope in anything;

dreams in my cubbyhole of a room where
the roaches scuttle from the tonguing gecko.

This music finds me giddy and centered, but when
morning comes, I am lost again, no love, just lost again.

Trickster IV

for Sister Patra

Surfing on the dance floor,
balancing that cut of wave,

missing brilliant coral with
a slash and sway of my arm,

watch me fall back, fall back,
then wheel and come again,

something catching me with
invisible hands on the downbeat.

Rapid is the chant of the microphone
queen with lyrics like a whip,

lashing me with her rhythm,
then balming me with a sweet

soprano sounding like sticky
on the bubbly bassline.

Sometimes the honey mellows in my soul
and melts my knees to water

and it's a sea surf teasing the sand
back and forth, making froth.

This, this, dis ya sound sweet
you see, sweet like sugar and lime.

Limbo is the way to limber,
seeming to fall back with my arms,

then catch me back with propeller action,
this is the Bogle at work, ya,

on the undulating salt deck of our days
to the sound we lost so long ago

when we left the kraal, leaving no forwarding
address, just forwarding to another rock.

But this echo of a land, a land
so far, so far, across the sea,

is lashed to the shock of this lyrical feast,
riding this sweet rhythmic beat.

Somebody say — Vershan! — and then hear
the drum in the sister's tongue,

playing like a gospeler to the wash
of the four-part harmony, dripping sex —

and the way I feel is wild;
wilding up myself with eyes open wide,

surfing on the dance floor
surfing on the dance floor.

And when she's done her lyrical jam
this rest is like old, old, old sleep

after sweating seawater, spilling seawater
flowing like that and falling: HEAVY!

Kingston Harbor

There is in Jacko's head an old memory
of a chaotic storm, flailing the Jamaican hills

with knife-blades of lightning and a silver
tumble of rain, pelting everything, pelting

him, beating his cowered head. And standing,
soaked to the skin, his neck veins jumping,

his hands gnarled with labor and seasoned
with the blood of slaughtered game,

his brows dripping like waterfalls
over his eyes, was Eric, disenfranchised,

staring after Jacko fleeing into the night;
Becky weeping, trying to shade her head

from the deluge with an old *Gleaner,* trying to
stay Eric's righteous hand, curled around the basic

wood of the machete, with her eyes, her eyes only.
Death, pale and bloodless, whispered among the trees,

and Jacko recalls the daring of Eric's
unflinching eyes. This memory returns

like seasonal storms, as clamorous
August's tropical depressions drive Jacko

and his sac full of blessed seed
into Kingston's harbor, then a slippery

point of departure, the sea, a buffer
against the coming of night, of dark night.

Now, Jacko stands staring into the island,
his back to the sea, his eyes cooled by the shadowing

hills, the purple hills of the Blue Mountains
shrouded in gray. He smiles at the way

the city glows against the ashen sky.
Jacko barrels gifts for his brother.

A peace offering to calm the years of resentment.
He can tell it will not be enough, not enough at all.

Requiem

1996

Research

...for me that was New York City, that was
where the pain was.

TOM FEELINGS

Tom Feelings,

You did not have to imagine
the masks of agony,
did not have to research
the eyes' blank stare,

Did not have to study ethnic tribes
to see the shape of Africa
in the lips and noses,
the weight of buttocks,

Did not have to invent
the blues of suffering,
the jazz of rebellion,
the fire of survival,

'Cause you looked across
Brooklyn and saw the road-weary
gaze of them who still travel
in the belly of ships,

Them who still sit among the cinder,
the soot, riding that freedom train
to the factories of the North
herded into the tombs of the ghetto;

Stared at your face in the mirror
after the stomach unfurls,

the skin smarting from being
spat on, shit on, pissed on.

You draw lines from somewhere cherished;
our gasps, groans, whispers
are the minor-keyed, antiphonal melodies
of our recognition of self.

We enter your holocaust
with trepidation and leave the stench
with tears, and something like gratitude
for the waters of healing, the salt, the light.

Swamp Poem

Sometimes, in the mist,
the artist can see the shape
of soldiers tense with waiting,
their guns at the ready.

The mist dries quickly
as the heat of the day comes,
and the artist is sitting
in the still of a swamp.

Outside Sumter, he buys boiled
groundnuts, feels his heart
thumping, his stomach heaving—
for a while there, in the mist,

he thought he smelled
the dank scent of kenke,
thought he was in Ghana
before the sun came.

Out of the lifting white
a boat glided by,
a woman, worn with age,
nodded her black head, passing.

The artist works quickly
in charcoals, fingers turning black,
eyes turning back to the swamp,
to the mist, to another life.

Requiem

I sing requiem
for the dead, caught in that
mercantilistic madness.

We have not built lasting
monuments of severe stone
facing the sea, the watery tomb,

so I call these songs
shrines of remembrance
where faithful descendants

may stand and watch the smoke
curl into the sky
in memory of those

devoured by the cold Atlantic.
In every blues I hear
riding the dank swamp

I see the bones
picked clean in the belly
of the implacable sea.

Do not tell me
it is not right to lament,
do not tell me it is tired.

If we don't, who will
recall in requiem
the scattering of my tribe?

In every reggae chant
stepping proud against Babylon
I hear a blue note

of lament, sweet requiem
for the countless dead,
skanking feet among shell,

coral, rainbow adze,
webbed feet, making as if
to lift, soar, fly into new days.

Language

Ashantis, Mandingoes, Ibos, Wolofs, Fulanis, Coromantees
Ashantis, Mandingoes, Ibos, Wolofs, Fulanis, Coromantees

Buried in the hill country,
the swamplands, the forests
of this New World oven
the words of tribes linger
like old mystery songs
tracing us back to something

Ashantis, Mandingoes, Ibos, Wolofs, Fulanis, Coromantees
Ashantis, Mandingoes, Ibos, Wolofs, Fulanis, Coromantees

Shame

If I heard the wail of a child,
over the lap of the sea,
heard the ebb of its whimpering,
eyes searching the void
for the familiar dark
of my face, my womb would burst,
my throat would open
and shatter the sky
with its scream.

They stand him
on wooden planks
to stare at the gawking heads
of men, too defiant
to make the passage to nowhere.
He stares, eyes tearing from the salt
in the humid air.
He must not hear me
stifling my moans,
numbing my flesh
from the stabbing
of those bloody penises.

At night
the creaking of the boat
lulls the tomb
and the babies,
chests weary with howling,
moan in reverie
while we lick our wounds,
wipe the wet from our thighs,
avert our gaze from the shame
of men, still alive, now boys,
witnesses to our abuse.

Warrior

I

Like a whip
unfurled,
his body
still taut
from sprinting
behind the fleeing elephant
gathers the ghost
and with a sudden plunge
guts the monster.
There is blood,
and the smell of bile.
The warrior
laughs, staring at the blood.
There is shock in his eyes
when they bring him down

II

Only to hoist
him up

III

Jerking,
jerking,
then still,
life is breathed out,
he dangles,
the warrior,
from the mast.

IV

Before you look
you smell
the swelling flesh;
the salt makes leather
of his skin;
flies nurtured
in the meat
mask the white
of his eyes.

V

You think
the rotting
will cause the neck
to give, but the skin
is now tough;
the rope
finds the grooves
of the spine,
hooks in.

VI

I see the thong
of his member
wither;
it falls.
The ghost
stares at the shrunken snake
as if staring at his own
manhood. Somebody laughs.

VII

It is hard now
to smell the canker.
The wind blows through
him like a flag.
The body is gutted
by the turning gulls.

The watch cries
Land!

VIII

I leave my heart
with the dangling warrior

I leave my heart
with the dangling warrior.

His teeth grin back
at me.

Land Ho

I cannot speak the languages
spoken in that vessel,
cannot read the beads
promising salvation.

I know this only,
that when the green of land
appeared like light
after the horror of this crossing,

we straightened our backs
and faced the simplicity
of new days with flame.
I know I have the blood of survivors

coursing through my veins;
I know the lament of our loss
must warm us again and again
down in the belly of the whale,

here in the belly of this whale
where we are still searching for homes.
We sing laments so old, so true,
then straighten our backs again.

Shook Foil

1997

Caution

The news comes like a stone:
cancer devoured his upful locks
and a sister collected the clumps
of carefully nurtured holiness
in a plastic bag to be matted
into a wig like a crown for the
bald Natty Dread in his casket.

He fell so low and the chemo seemed
like treachery. It all turned
worthless, this fighting, this
scramble for a cure, a way out;
this confession of mortality:

O Jah, O Jah, why has thou
forsaken thy son? O Jah,

the veil is black like this night,
black like the treacherous road;

when it wet it slippery,
see me sliding, tumbling down;

see how this sickness make my soul
black as jet, caution, caution,

and my brothers, all they can say
is walk, walk, walk, walk, walk,

like the bubbling syncopations
of the synthesizer's left-hand jumps.

But who will walk with me,
who will carry the lamp on this path,

whose breathing will reassure me
of a company waiting on the other side?

My brethren will forsake me,
I walk into so many dark places
while I wait for the coming of light.

Reggae rides the airwaves
and this island sound dark
for the passing of a song.

Natural

for Bob Marley

In the silence, the silence of
a new void of morning, I taste
the bitter weed of loss, like mauby,
like a forerunner to my own loss —
staring at the open autopsied corpse
of the body that housed my father,
lamenting only that which may have been,
lamenting that sometimes we die
before poetic justice can mete its magic:
Oh the things that could have been!
The dead young are impossible equations.
Morning, morning, I walk along the leaf-strewn
avenues of the campus, a sun-specked
day; the blessed light on my upturned face
making me think of the confession you made
at Cane River where on the rocks you laid your head,
there in desolate places to make your bed,
to make music; I find the stones here
take to the alchemy of poetry so well.
I walk like a poet in search of remembrances.
The slip of my memory gathers images
and tosses them among the turning leaves
to let fall something like rain
on a blazing hot day, rainwater touching
soft asphalt and making steam as sweet
and reassuring as incense in the sanctuary.

Silent

I

The picky-picky headed ten-year-olds
   throw down gigs whose nails
chew into the flesh of the earth.
   In the dust storm, the children
are unmoved, they become one color,
   they return to their origins.
I watch and imagine an eternity
   in this conceit: dust to dust.
I let the ash turn then settle in my mind.
   My purity is no longer intact —
it lasted for months; I lived
   in this pristine place of devotion,
where my mind was blocked to every
   wayward sound. The music of the city,
I blocked; the sound of voices, warm
   in the steamy nights, I blocked;
the pounding of my heart in dreams
   of laughing women, I blocked;
the trigger of anger and the orgasm
   of its flaming, I blocked;
till in this monk silence, I found power.

II

Celibacy, I find, breeds a mind
as clear as Augustine's stark cubicle.
   It is true. My old sins come
on the wave of music. Debauchery is a sound.
   I find my mouth filled with red noises,
and then the fall is irrevocable.

This is why I have run toward the vacuum
of silence, not to hear, but to not hear.
   Watching the boys in their mute dance
cloaked in the turning dust, I understand epiphany,
   I understand the silence of piety.
Afterward, the open lot is dotted
   by flowering pox with delicate
rims of the finest sand where the gigs have spun.
   Entering the void of their departure
is like entering a chapel of red hues.
   I study the silence, restored again, renewed.

Shook Foil

The whole earth is filled with the love of God.
   In the backwoods, the green light
is startled by blossoming white petals,
   soft pathways for the praying bird
dipping into the nectar, darting in starts
   among the tangle of bush and trees.
My giddy walk through this speckled grotto
   is drunk with the slow mugginess
of a reggae bassline, finding its melody
   in the mellow of the soft earth's breath.
I find the narrow stream like a dog sniffing,
   and dip my sweaty feet in the cool.
While sitting in this womb of space
   the salad romantic in me constructs a poem. This is all I
      can muster
   before the clatter of schoolchildren
searching for the crooks of guava branches
   startles all with their expletives and howls;
the trailing snot-faced child wailing perpetual —
   with ritual pauses for breath and pity.
In their wake I find the silver innards of discarded
   cigarette boxes, the anemic pale of tossed
condoms, the smashed brown sparkle of Red Stripe
   bottles, a mélange of bones and rotting fruit,
there in the sudden white light of noon.

II

   How quickly the grandeur fades into a poem,
how easily everything of reverie starts to crumble.
   I walk from the stream. Within seconds
sweat soaks my neck and back; stones clog my shoes,

88

flies prick my flaming face and ears,
bramble draws thin lines of blood on my arms.
    There is a surfeit of love hidden here;
at least this is the way faith asserts itself.
    I emerge from the valley of contradictions,
my heart beating with the effort, and stand looking
    over the banking, far into Kingston Harbor
and the blue into gray of the Caribbean Sea.
    I dream up a conceit for this journey
and with remarkable snugness it fits;
    this reggae sound: the bluesy mellow
of a stroll on soft, fecund earth, battling the crack
    of the cross-stick; the scratch of guitar,
the electronic manipulation of digital sound,
    and the plaintive wail of the grating voice.
With my eyes closed, I am drunk with the mellow,
    swimming, swimming among the green of better days;
and I rise from the pool of sound, slippery with
    the warm cling of music on my skin,
and enter the drier staleness of the road
    that leads to the waiting city of fluorescent lights.

Prayer for My Son

for Keli

I

When the moist sores sucked strength from your
    frail limbs, I cried out.
Healing came in gradual waves and then you smiled.
    Still, I lie with my silence,
no testimony on my lips, no rejoicing,
    no credit given. I lie.
And there are the days
    of waiting for the wrath to fall,
my punishment for ingratitude,
    collecting miracles like a blooming tree
collects birds, but hides the blossoms
    in skirts of modest green.
Trees have shriveled for less.
    It is written.
This is the quicksand of Babylon,
    dwelling in this place of stagnant logic.
I find even the magic of poems to be forced.
    I live and eat with a people
of calculating guile, who can't see the light
    of a jeweled night for the orange
glow of fluorescent bulbs. When I testify
    in their midst, they fidget
at the gaucheness of my passion, then adroitly
    make humor and little of my faith.

II

These days I barely hear my supplicant moan
    under cover of my dreams.
When morning comes, I quickly forget,

for how can I expect the magic
of healing when my tongue will not
    speak it, proclaim it, herald it?
I wait for the fire to burn the chafe
    as I watch my child's limbs heal.
It is all I can muster in this barren
    place. My last cry will be
a plea for the unfurling of my tongue
    to draw new paths
in this land of the mute and doubting.
    My last prayer spoken,
I wait for the bright miracle to flame
    in the twilight of peace,
between night and morning, when dew
    is lavender scented and cool,
when the sky is russet soft
    with bated hope.

Shadow Play

for Akua

Morning birds play shadow games
on my pink light-filtering louvers,
    swoops of grays against the light.
Akua sips the air delicately,
    her eyes fluttering to the moving shadow
of the falling birds; her fists curl,
    punch harmlessly into the air,
while whistles, caws, peeps and squeals
    of birds and insects lull the morning.
My devotions are easier here,
    meditations on the preciousness of life;
I want to swallow, embrace,
    become one with every peace
that suggests itself in the pink and white
    of this morning's communion.
I can believe in miracles in this place.
    My daughter breathes a sigh,
groans, and when I turn from
    the shadow play, her eyes are glittering,
wide open and reading music
    floating in ribbons across the silence.
In her eyes are centuries of seeing,
    as if she has seen all this before,
lived it all before, and sung of it before.
    Before she cries out, I gather her up,
still surprised at the lightness, the bird-like
    vulnerability of her warm, soft body.
She breathes, and breathes and breathes
    like a mantra for new mornings.

Rita

I

I first saw you cooking in the background
of a jumpy camera shot, while the dread
held forth, constructing his facade of enigma,
dodging the barbs and darts of Babylon with code,
and three times he denied you, called you a sister,
like Isaac did to Rebekah, leaving her there,
hanging like that, open season for Abimelech
and the boys, that is what you were,
a flower tarnished, just a helping sister,
Martha in the kitchen swollen with child.
And who, watching this, would have known
of the nights he would crawl into your carbolic
womb, to become the man-child again,
searching for a father who rode off on his white steed
and never returned, never sent a message?

II

For years I thought you had lied,
for it was our way to believe the patriarch,
and who would want to declare the coupling
of the downtown dread with the uptown Miss World,
too sweetly ironic, too much of Hollywood
in this sun-drenched, dust-beaten city?
Who would let your black face, weighed by the insult,
disturb our reverie? I did not believe the rumors.
So while the nation grumbled and cussed you out,
declared you gold digger and such the like
when he was buried and celebrated in death,
and you published the wedding photos,
the family snapshots of another time;

when you battled like a higgler for rights,
and played every dubious game in the book,
roughhouse, slander, ratchet smile and all,
I called it poetic, the justice you received,
for you played the cards right, no bad card drawn
in your hands, as you sat quietly in the back room
like a nun, bride of Christ and slave to mission.
And when you knew other men
before the tears could dry from our eyes,
and made another child in your fertile womb,
when your garments of silence were replaced
with the garish gold and silver of decadence,
when you entered the studio to play rude girl,
naughty as hell, talking about feeling damned high,
and rolling your backside like a teenager,
I had to smile at the poetic meaning of it all,
for you fasted before this feast,
you played the wife of noble character
eating the bitter fruit of envy
while the dread sought out the light-skinned
beauties, from London to L.A., King Solomon
multiplying himself among the concubines.

III

These days I have found a lesson of patience
in your clever ways, a picture of fortitude
despite the tears — you are Jamaican woman,
with the pragmatic walk of a higgler,
offering an open bed for his mind-weary nights,
an ear for his whispered fears and trepidations,
and a bag of sand for a body to be beaten,
slapped up, kicked and abused; you took it all,
like a loan to be paid in full at the right time.
I no longer blame you for the rabid battles
raging over the uneasy grave of the rhygin dread;

for now I know how little we know of those
salad days in a Saint Ann's farmer's one-room shack,
where you made love like a stirring pot,
and watched the stars — for they were the only light.
What potions you must have made to tie, tie
your souls together like this! I simply watch
your poetic flight, black sister, reaping fruit
for the mother left abandoned with a fair-skinned child,
for the slave woman who caressed the head
of some married white master, with hopes
of finding favor when the days were ripe,
all who sucked salt and bitter herbs,
all who scratched dust, scavenged for love,
all who drew bad cards; you have
walked the walk well. The pattern is an old one.
I know it now. It's your time now, daughter.
Ride on, natty dread, ride on, my sister, ride on.

Midland

2001

Inheritance

O Christ, my craft, and the long time it is taking!
DEREK WALCOTT

I

In the shade of the sea grape trees the air is tart
with the sweet and sour of stewed fruit rotting
about his sandaled feet. His skin,
still Boston pale and preserved with Brahmin
devotion by the hawkish woman
who smells cancer in each tropical wind,
is caged in shadows. I know those worn eyes,
their feline gleam, mischief-riddled;
his upper lip lined with a thin stripe
of tangerine, the curled-up nervousness
of a freshly shaved mustache. He is old
and cared for. He accepts mashed food
though he still has teeth — she insists, and love
is about atoning for the guilt
of those goatish years in New England.
A prophet's kind of old. Old like casket-
aged genius. Above, a gull surveys
the island, stitches loops through the sea and sky —
an even horizon, the bias on which
teeters a landscape, this dark loam of tradition
in which seeds split into tender leaves.

II

The smudge of colors spreads and dries in the sun.
The pulpy paper sucks in the watercolor,
and the cliché of sea and a fresh beach
seems too easy for a poem. He has written
them all, imagined the glitter and clatter
of silver cuirasses, accents of crude
Genoese sailors poisoning the air,
the sand feeling for the first time the shadow
of flag and plumed helmet—this old story
of arrival that stirred him as a boy,
looking out over the open plains,
as he cluttered the simple island
with the intrigues of blood and heroes,
his gray eyes searching out an ancestry
beyond the broad laughter and breadfruit-
common grunts of the fishermen, pickled
with rum and the *picong* of *kaiso,*
their histories as shallow as the trace
of soil at the beach's edge where crippled
corn bushes have sprouted. That was years ago;
he has now exhausted the jaundiced language
of a broken civilization.
These days he just chips at his epitaph,
a conceit of twilights turning into
bare and bleak nights. He paints, whistling
Sparrow songs while blistering in the sun.

III

The note pad, though, is not blank. The words start,
thirteen syllables across the page, then seven
before the idea hesitates. These days
he does not need to count, there is in his head
a counter dinging an alarm like the bell
of his old Smith Corona. His line breaks
are tidy dramas of his entrances
and exits, he will howl before the darkness.
This ellipsis is the tease of a thought,
the flirtatious lift of a yellow skirt
showing a brown taut thigh — a song he knows
how to hum but can't recall the lyrics, man —
an airy metaphor — taken up
by a flippant sea breeze going someplace
inland, carrying the image, snagged
by the olive-dull entanglement
of a thorny patch. At eight he lays
the contents of his canvas book bag
on the sand, organizing the still life
like honed stanzas. He scoops the orange pulp
of papaya, relishing the taste of fruit, this bounty
harvested from the ant-infested fragile tree
that bleeds each time its fruit is plucked.
The flesh is sunny. He knows the fishermen warn
it will cut a man's nature, dry up
his sap; that women feed their men pureed
papaya in tall glasses of rum-punch
to tie them down, beached, benign pirogues
heading nowhere. He dares the toxins
to shrivel him, to punish him
for the chronic genius of crafting poems
from the music of a woman's laugh
while he chews slowly. A poem comes to him
as they sometimes do in the chorus

of a song. It dances about in his head.
He does not move to write it down — it will wait
if it must, and if not, it is probably
an old sliver of long-discarded verse.

IV

The old men in the rum shop are comforted
as they watch him limp along the gravel
road, wincing at the sharp prod of stones
in his tender soles, the knees grinding
at each sudden jar — just another ancient
recluse with his easel folded under
his arm, a straw hat, the gull-gray eyes
seeing the sea before he clears the hill.
They know him, proud of the boy — bright as hell
and from good people. There is no shared language
between them, just the babel of rum talk
and cricket sometimes. Under his waters
he talks of Brussels, Florence, barquentines,
Baudelaire, rolling the words around
like a cube of ice — they like to hear
the music he makes with his tongue; the way
he tears embracing this green island,
this damned treasure, this shit hole of a treasure.
Sometimes if you don't mind sharp, you would think
him white, too, except for the way him hold
him waters, carry his body against the sun
with the cool, cultivated calm of a rumhead.
Him say home like it come from a book;
hard to recognize when him say home
that is this dry beachhead and tired earth
him talking. They like it, anyway, the way
they like to hear "Waltzing Matilda" sung
with that broad Baptist harmony to a *cuatro*
plunked, to hear it fill an old song night.

V

If he is my father (there is something
of that fraying dignity, and the way
genius is worn casual and urbane — aging
with grace) he has not lost much over the years.
The cigarette still stings his eyes and the scent
of Old Spice distilled in Gordon's Dry Gin
is familiar here by the sea where a jaunty
chantey, the cry of gulls, and the squeak
of the rigging of boats are a right backdrop—
but I have abandoned the thought, the search
for my father in this picture. He's not here,
though I still come to the ritual deathwatch
like a vulture around a crippled beast,
the flies already bold around its liquid
eyes, too resigned to blink. I have come
for the books, the cured language, the names
of this earth that he has invented,
the stories of a town, and the way
he finds women's slippery parts in the smell
and shape of this island, the making
and unmaking of a city through
the epic cataclysm of fire,
eating old brittle wood, myths dancing
in the thick smoke like the gray ashen debris
of sacrifice. It is all here with him —
this specimen living out his twilight days,
prodigious as John's horror — the green
uncertain in the half-light. When we meet
he is distant, he knows I want to draw
him out, peer in for clues. He will not be drawn out,
he is too weary now. He points his chin
to the rum shop, to an old man, Afolabe
sitting on the edge of a canoe, black
as consuming night. I can tell
that he carries a new legend in his terrible
soul each morning, a high tower over the sea.

VI

I could claim him easily, make of him
a tale of nurture and benign neglect;
he is alive, still speaks, his brain clicks
with the routine of revelations
that can spawn in me the progeny
of his monumental craft. These colonial
old men, fed on cricket and the tortured
indulgences of white schoolmasters
patrolling the mimic island streets
like gods growing gray and sage-like in the heat
and stench of the third world; they return
to the reactionary nostalgia
during their last days — it is the manner
of aging, we say, but so sad, so sad.
I could adopt him, dream of blood and assume
his legacy of a divided self.
But it would ring false quickly; after all
my father saw the Niger eating out
a continent's beginnings; its rapid
descent to the Atlantic; he tasted
the sweet *kelewele* of an Akan
welcome, and cried at the uncompromising
flame of *akpetechi*. The blood of his sons
was spilled like libation into the soil, and more:
in 1926, an old midwife
buried his bloodied navel string, and the afterbirth
of his arrival, at the foot of an ancient
cotton tree there on the delta islands
of Calabar. My blood defines the character
of my verse. Still, I pilfer (a much better word),
rummage through the poet's things to find the useful,
how he makes a parrot flame a line
or a cicada scream in wind; the names
he gives the bright berries of an island
in the vernacular of Adam and the tribe.

VII

I carry the weight of your shadow always,
while I pick through your things for the concordance
of your invented icons for this archipelago.
Any announcement of your passing
is premature. So to find my own strength,
I seek out your splendid weaknesses.
Your last poems are free of the bombast
of gaudy garments, I can see the knobs
of your knees scarred by the surgeon's incisions
to siphon water and blood from bone;
I stare at your naked torso — the teats
hairy, the hint of a barreled beauty
beneath the folding skin. I turn away
as from a mirror. I am sipping your blood,
tapping the aged sap of your days while you grow
pale. You are painting on the beach, this is how
the poem began — I am watching you watching
the painting take shape. I have stared long enough
that I can predict your next stroke — your dip
into the palette, your grunts, your contemplative
moments, a poised crane waiting for the right
instance to plunge and make crimson ribbons
on a slow-moving river. These islands
give delight, sweet water with berries,
the impossible theologies
of reggae, its metaphysics so right
for the inconstant seasons of sun and muscular
storm — you can hear the shape of a landscape
in the groan of the wind against the breadfruit
fronds. I was jealous when at twenty, I found
a slim volume of poems you had written
before you reached sixteen. It has stitched in me
a strange sense of a lie, as if all this
will be revealed to be dust — as if I learned
to pretend one day, and have yet to be found out.

Holy Dub

> ...round
> my mud hut I hear again
>
> the cry of the lost
> swallows, horizons' halloos, found-
> ationless voices, voyages
>
> KAMAU BRATHWAITE

I

Let us gather, then, the legend of faith,
truth of our lives in this crude foment of days.

We are so afraid to look to the sky, so cowed, we whisper
of straight paths while a nation grows fat on its own flesh.

Our gospel — our testament — makes martyrs of us.
Another life,
scribbles the scribe, his parchment sucking the blood
of root dyes.

We keep these hymns we've sung through time as stations of our journeys.

Come to the waters
There is a vast supply,
There is a river,
That never shall run dry.
Hallelujah!

II

His afro recedes, creeping toward the nape creaturely,
his forehead is a veined, leathered casing.

The lamplight is guarded by the soot-stained,
wafer-thin glass, with its simple web of doilies

in pale yellow paint — such basic
craft, such splendor in useful things.

He is writing himself into a brittle savanna,
and the mother's calm song he hears is the meaning of faithfulness.

Too-too bobbii
Too-too bobbii.

Her sound carries for miles while her choleric
child fatigues the night with a wailing counterpoint.

The remembrance of old blood makes his skin
accept the sun. The livery is long burnished.

The music of lullabies turns about the poet's head.
His skin has grown darker here — *obroni* black man.

He speaks Ewe, understands the pidgin of mosquitoes.

III

Between click-filled night and pink dawn,
Beethoven's miserable lament

circles the bungalow that squats beneath the naked
mesh of a *yoyi*'s canopy. He finds comfort

in this music, so like the orange dry of the grasslands,
the deep blues of memory. In the symphony's turn

is a thick sweetness of cheap wine and the substance
of fresh bread, still warm, broken by rough hands.

He records the gospel of the desert people,
poor folk whose mornings are oblations to light.

This poet is a griot in search of a village. He will forget
all dreams come sunlight. He fears this most.

For decades they will remain myths of a better life,
until he reaches the wilderness of his last dawns,

in a too-cold loft over Greenwich Village where he will
try to make verse like they used to make psalms:

to last and last.

Satta: En Route to Columbia, S.C.

I-Roy rides the gap
where the sax used to rest
and the bass talking
to the Royal man who
can turn a rhyme into sacredness

Want to chant damnation
where my enemies gawk
at the tumbling enjambments
ramming home a truth

Who who who can say
concubine! like tracing
out the wicked's path to hell
like I-Royal, mouth shooting fire?

So, *satta a massa*
says the prophet
cool like a knife-edge
and then catch the cross-
stick tacking a rhythm
satta a massa gana

I am striding through an alien
landscape, the road smooth
the air heavy with rain
and my heart bluesing along
when the prophet speaks
and it is enough for the grooves
of a forty-five's glimmering vinyl
the comfort of God again on me

Look into the book of life and you will see
that there's a land far far away

110

Midland

for Krystal

A Letter from Greeleyville

Dear Claudia:
Few things here succumb to time though the old grow tender
and die. Still, they appear again in the new light,
same face, same open skirts, same fingers clutching pipes
smoking a halo about their heads, rocking a blues on the same porches.
You would like this place for a time, but I know you would long
for the clean efficiency of your city — the stench of manufactured age.
The stench of jasmine and the dank earthiness of this soil
soaked by an old river, so long silted by the runoff
of a generation of fears, detritus, and funky bundles
of hair, sin, phlegm, blood passed out each month,
shoved, clumped, burned into the blooming ground, remind me
of Sturge Town in Saint Ann where my grandfather is buried
in a thick grotto of aloe vera and stunted pimento trees.
But this place speaks a language I have to learn, and this woman
who travels with me introduces me to the earth and her folks
as a stranger, a specimen from far away, I pretend I do not feel
the welling of tears when I smell the old sweat of her grandmother's
housedress hanging from a nail on the back of an oak door.
The corn has turned a rotten gold and pale in the summer,
the twine of leaves and roots dark and spotted while the mildewed glory
of old hymnals seeps from the Saint James Baptist church
where the blues have marinated the boards till they are supple
with the fluent pliability of faith so old it knows the ways of God
like it knows family, and blood ties. I am stealing things from here
and sending them to you, knowing you are too decent to use them.
But do, keep them safe till I arrive for a spell, and then I will find
good use for these sweet collectibles, lasting things. Love, Kwame.

Blues on Route 15 with Krystal

At midmorning, we watch the green of tobacco stanzas,
such even reckoning of this state where a nation carved its name
into Cherokee country, making a new landscape: plows turning the earth
to the slow assured cadence of the Baptist hymns, the rebel yells,
the scalper's knife. Yet there is something tender here.

We are riding Route 15 through Manning toward Kingstree,
searching for Alma's meditation on home in the sweetly pained
bourbon-grooved voice of Lady Day that Krystal plays
again and again, punching viciously at the knobs, rushing the tape
back to its beginning. And Lady Day conjures the skeletal twist of an oak
somewhere where the torture of fear and the faraway cry of the dead
are the same, despite the tundra cold. Krystal points to a green bluff,
a tree isolated against an indifferent blue sky — *Like that,* she says.
The common trees, the quality of light in the sky. I sat under that tree
once — I don't remember why, but we sat there, me and my mother,
and we ate sandwiches, and she was crying for no good reason.

III

In Search of Alma

After the storm, the ravaging of the earth,
the stripping of green, the pounding of winds
on tender flesh; after the howling,
the green grows hungrily over everything,
and how quickly the multitude of sins
is covered by the crawling of wisteria and kudzu.
This earth speaks no memories of wrongs done;
there is a sweet politeness here, a way of decency,
the value of perfume in damp kerchiefs outside
the outhouse where the flies buzz rudely.

I have come to seek out Alma's lament,
to scratch into her grave, and find the rot,
of crumbling softness that was her paler self.

IV

Crow over Corn Row

Above the shock of cotton trees hangs a solitary
bird, against the sky. It is black and stays only long enough
to seem like a portent. Standing in the cotton groves, I pluck
the coarse filthy white tangle from the gray brittle unlipping
of the flower. There is nothing like the hint of a vulva's softness here;
all juice dried out, the earth gives up its beaten self
in the language of simple cotton, the tight tangle
of the squat bushes, the debris from years of shedding
upturned like the unexpected shallow graves
of massacred millions. I pluck at the stubborn seeds
until the ball of cotton is softer in my palm.
The bird swoops, turns, and fades into the blue.
This short peace defies the rustle of old ghosts
quarreling in the twisted ribbons of the corn leaves.
It is hard to breathe in this heat and stench, easier to drive on,
the wind cupped by the car, warm relief on a wet body.

V

Roosting

I drive toward the burned-out Baptist church
with its well-kept graveyard — green, flowered —
and blackened walks desecrated with familiar
hatred, hieroglyphs of a twisted myth.

*"You have just received a courtesy call from the knights
of the Ku Klux Klan. Don't make the next be a business call."*

I remember the bird, black as a crow
or raven chattering over the cacophony of corn,
uncertain of a place to land, so he moved on.

But the symbol is too convenient — too balanced.

Now a flock of audacious crows stare
into the gutted sanctuary, shaded by the fresh
whiteness of blooming dogwood.
They are roosting, as if they have found a place to haunt,
as if the feet of some long-forgotten dead
were shod with shoes for walking by ignorant folks,
as if no one's head is pointed east to home.

I keep a piece of burnt timber as a souvenir,
my fingers growing black with soot.
The silence prays over me.

VI

Decent Folk

A voice, high as a countertenor, shatters the eaves;
the aria of a storm twists its path through
the thick peach groves of this blood-soaked land
high like a castrato gallivanting through
a Handel requiem, a lament for the dead;
this sound is bearded, broad-chested, and cynical,
it is ripping through the state, now, seasoned
by the warmth of Florida's serrated coastline,
and the family gathers to whisper prayers as the world
crumbles around them. The blackness is heavy.
They pass down their stories to the wail of death
warding off the tears with the preserved narratives
of survival. What they speak are lies, the truths
are entombed secrets, the ritual secrets of rural folk,
still decent enough to know that talking about
love between that cracker Buddy Lawrence
and Powie, sweet Powie, is sacrilege, sinful,
plain indecent. No one thinks to ask how
twelve babies, yellow and pink, came howling
from that smoky womb. No one thinks to ask
how come he dies there in the house he built
for her, the wind blowing like it is now,
and the next generation staring at this man,
this white man breathing his last right under
the flared nostrils of Jimmy Crow. No one asks
nothing. Powie was raped, is all. The rest
is silence and the dignity of black folks
cultivated on this equivocal land, the rows
even, the time of harvest arriving like the moon,
relentless, the way it has always been, always will be.

VII

Epoch

"I moan this way 'cause he's dead," she said.
"Then tell me, who is that laughing upstairs?"
"Them's my sons. They glad."

RALPH ELLISON, *INVISIBLE MAN*

Krystal, an epoch glows beneath your skin.
Your nose spreads like flattened clay, your lips,
bloody grapefruit, wet, startled crimson.
You hurried your makeup, and the base is too pale
for your skin. You have no time for the paletting,
the mixing of hues to find the dialect of your history.
There is the epoch of silence in your skin,
something hidden, a curse in the long of your lower back
before the deviance of your buttocks.
A family of tangerine people; your folk are black,
thoroughly African, southern folk shaped in the kerosene-smelling
back quarters, where old pork was cured; at night, the flies, groggy,
drunk with the heat, and Buddy Lawrence panting into this soil,
this tendon-tight woman, making babies with transparent skin.
Powie begat Alma begat Okla begat Lynne begat Krystal: the years
do not seem enough between the ash and tar of a Sumter lynching
and the promise of better days. Your skin does not trust its language
of appeasement. You stand in the stark sun, trying to darken your skin,
but it grows transparent in the heat, and all is palimpsest,
the language of blood underneath your skin.

VIII

To the Third and Fourth Generations

You too carry the soup of nausea, the taste of a man's forced breath
behind you, the crawl of his hands cupping at your flesh,
the thought of dreaming your face into the wide spaces of low country
where the bandy-legged, tobacco-chewing cliché of a farmer came
        to find
the perfect lip and tongue of your ancestor. Still, at night,
you dream his head, too heavy for the smallness of his body,
his tiny hands open, trying to touch your nipple.
And you wish for an instant that he were the cracker, Buddy Lawrence,
so you could, for Powie, for Alma, for the host of mothers, leave
        him castrated
and bleeding in the half-light. But his hair kinks, his eyes are black
as Elmina's dungeons, and his smile reeks of the disarming sweet of a
        Motown song.
You will not write this down. You will store it quietly, like Powie did,
trusting that the ruined cells will seed in another womb, another
        generation
free enough to speak the genetic vernacular of anger.

IX

Somebody Trouble the Water

Wade in the water
Wade in the water, children
Wade in the water...

In a dream, I am in the Sahara with its tongue of heat
on the edges of Egypt. The sand is carnelian, stained with old
     sacrificial pots.
The shards are all that remain. It has been centuries and still,
in the early morning, a girl walks slowly, the soft sand slipping under
     her feet;
a smudge of white flutters in her hands rippled by the wind's lick.
On a perfectly smooth rock, she batters the tender dove,
its blood gleaming on the stone. She pulls out the soft viscera
and reads them while the new sun splatters the mountain's face.
She is a dream so distant she seems worth forgetting.
But she changes, as dreams tend to, and it is you, Krystal, who
     stands there,
over the grave of Alma, this time, your palms open, the wet
     tissue speckled
by the green above you. You have been crying, making, I can tell,
unreasonable covenants with the dead, with the living,
with the mountains at your back in this place of silence.
This South's sores are still too fresh. A hand plunged
into the earth will touch the sticky moisture of its brokenness.
You've got to sing those songs just to keep on keeping on, Krystal.

Wade in the water
Wade in the water, children
Wade in the water
God's gonna trouble the water
God's gonna trouble the water.

Bruised Totems

2004

Bruised Totems

The air is clean
sterilizing the stories
once sweated
into the wood, terra-cotta,
ivory, and bone.

We have only orderly shelves
with off-white tags
numbered in a woman's hand
dangling on thin threads.

They are arrayed neatly,
these stiff masks,
a host of holy witnesses
so far away from the humid
air of home.

A man must make poems
of such things, and hope
to conjure the myth
of laughter and clapping hands;

the bruised totems
of a civilization.

Mask

First shape the wood,
burn out its pulpy guts,
leave the hollowed shell
a thin skin of hard wood.

Shine light through the slits
for eyes, so the green and sky
rising above the red dirt
will burn through.

The grate of teeth
for the spirit to chew
and the hole of a nose
for it to breathe
the sweet offerings
burned on aromatic balsam,
must be cut out of the wood.

Then place tiny plates of copper,
armor to protect
the vulnerable forehead
of the dancer, so that no rot,
no rut can destroy dreams
of the nation in her head.

We find the mask,
wear her to see our fears,
to dance into days
clean as infant song.

Gallery Art

Ripped from the rooted trunk,
your body stands, staunch,
in perpetual pout.

Oh sister, your knob navel
is a rough screw in your skin.

I come to witness the coy
of your body, now cleaned up
in the open gallery guarded
by a curator who warns
that my breath on you
may cause you to crumble,
your parts to fall away.

Oh sister, we are a long way
from home, you and I.

Sight

for Rwanda

Every ax should have an eye
to see the havoc
that it wreaks.

These days our tools are made
in factories. Machetes
blind as stone arrive
stacked high in trucks.

They do not see
the soft eyes
of a child.

Every ax must have an eye
to see the havoc
that it wreaks.

Gourd

The browned gourd
carries the echo of music

like the taste of garden eggs and okra stew
with its slivers of white river fish
with its crimson peppers

islanding a mound of pounded cassava.
The browned gourd
is the pregnant fullness

of a woman's belly,
the sounds of its water
the suck-suck of an infant
the hum of deep water
when you pluck a string.

Trace your fingers up the neck
that ends at the rigid head of dignity—
how she organizes the notes
before they zither down the strings
into the dense dreams.

The browned gourd
is a woman's breast

with the babel of truth
uncertain as a voice
searching for healing in song;
uncertain as a poem
before it arrives with words.

Brimming

2006

Dreaming of Saint Augustine

Stono Rebellion, South Carolina, 1739

At dawn, the mist settles on our skin.
We are sweating through the thick underbrush.
Ahead, light is the ghost of hope;
behind, the darkness is shelter.
We are running south toward the river,
hoping to find the shallow crossing
where the dense forest near the border
is the hope of freedom. We are running
leaving behind the splatter of blood,
the prayers of the saints, the stench
of rum, the howl of dogs, the clamor
of our chains. Savannah River whispers
in the silence. We baptize our faces
with a handful of Spanish moss,
suck the water from the tendrils,
then run, keep running, hoping
for the sound *Saint Augustine,*
for the language we have long
forgotten; for a gentle, gentle sleep.

after Brian Rutenberg's *Spanish Moss*

How to Pick a Hanging Tree

Pastoral scene of the gallant south,
The bulging eyes and the twisted mouth,
Scent of magnolias, sweet and fresh,
Then the sudden smell of burning flesh.

LEWIS ALLAN

Young trees may look sturdy, but they have no memory,
they are green so near the surface they bend with sudden weight;
and the truth is that not all trees can carry a man's dead weight
with enough air between pointed toes and earth, with enough height
so the scent of rotting can carry far enough to be a message
for those who are sniffing the muggy air for news.

Old as it may look, craggy bark, twisted branches,
drooping limbs, old as it may seem sitting there by the edge
of the canal, that live oak understands the simple rituals of hanging.
See, there is the natural notch where the rope will slip,
and hold, and here, the tree angled like this, the damp air
off the river carries the decay for miles and miles.

Sometimes, a fresh tree will simply die after the piss
of a dying man seeps into its roots. Sometimes a tree
will start to rot from guilt or something like a curse.
But the old trees, seasoned by the flame of summer lightning,
and hardened to tears, know it is nothing to be a tree, mute
and heartless, just strong enough to carry a man until he turns to air.

after Brian Rutenberg's *Shade*

Brimming

A silken veil, this light rain
softens the flaming oak leaves.

The tarmac is gleaming wet.
God on the black river's belly.

Deep at night, the rain lifts;
a cool breeze tickles my skin,

dries sweat and the dew's mist.
Naked, I slip through the woods.

A new fist of cloud crowds the west;
I stand, head thrown back and open-mouthed.

after Brian Rutenberg's Waccamaw #28

Graves

After the light-colored shallows,
the deep river is our resting place.

We plunge into the chill;
everything is black down here.

Staring upward: the sky
glows in mists of green and silver.

Below, the riverbed undulates
like a drought-burned prairie.

Deeper, the smooth shoulder
of a sudden valley glows yellow.

We find the skulls of simple folk
buried in the broken graveyard

on the slopes of a village
lost to the floodwaters of a trained

river; we find a brick crucifix,
and the sound of prayers murmuring

in the dark belly of this river.
When we come up for air

the boat has drifted far down-
stream, and a soft rain is falling.

after Brian Rutenberg's Irish Painting #15

Carolina Gold

for Brian Rutenberg

Hurl me through memory
and I will return panting
with my satchel filled
with the stories strangers
tell me at the crossroads.

In the low country
it takes just a few years
for a storm's scars to heal,
for the moss and thickets
to cover crumbled stones.

In the low country
a forest covers a multitude
of sins, and we make camp
humming, trying not to hear
the clamor underfoot.

If you walk barefoot
through the forest, you will
feel the dip and swell
of old graves, how near
the surface is the water table.

Words such as *beauty*
are the artist's hope, but
his dreams are of terror
and the testing of light —
the language of color.

I walk through this hall
and find myself tossed
from light to light,
and it is hard to breathe,
hard to stop to look.

Outside, the sudden light
of Columbia in July
is strange comfort.
I make blood poems
before I sleep.

after Brian Rutenberg's *Carolina Gold*

Wisteria

2006

Wisteria

Circumspect woman,
you carry your memories
tied up in a lipstick-stained
kerchief in a worn straw basket.
When you undo the knot,
the scent of wisteria,
thick with the nausea of nostalgia,
fills the closed-in room.

You lean into the microphone,
smile at the turning tape
while fingering the fading petals.
You intone your history,
breathing in the muggy
scent of wayward love.
You anger is always
a whisper, enigmatic,
almost unspoken,
just a steady heat.

I don't like 'em
never did, never could...

Tornado Child

for Rosalie Richardson

I am a tornado child.
I come like a swirl of black
and darken up your day;
I whip it all into my womb,
lift you and your things,
carry you to where you've never been
and maybe, if I feel good,
I might bring you back,
all warm and scared,
heart humming wild like a bird
after early sudden flight.

I am a tornado child.
I tremble at the elements.
When thunder rolls
my mother-womb trembles,
remembering the tweak of contractions
that tightened to a wail
when my mother pushed me out
into the black of a tornado night.

I am a tornado child,
you can tell us from far,
by the crazy of our hair;
couldn't tame it if we tried.
Even now I tie a bandanna
to silence the din of anarchy
in these coir-thick plaits.

I am a tornado child
born in the whirl of clouds;
the center crumbled,
then I came. My lovers
know the blast
of my chaotic giving;
they tremble at the whip
of my supple thighs;
tornado child—you cross me
at your peril—I cling to light
when the warm of anger
lashes me into a spin,
the pine trees bend to me
swept in my gyrations.

I am a tornado child.
When the spirit takes my head,
I hurtle into the vacuum
of white sheets billowing
and paint a swirl of color,
streaked with my many songs.

Black Funk

The rigid of my jawbone
is power forged in the oven
of every blow I have felt.
My water walk is something like
compensation for a limp.
Don't begrudge me my sashay
walk, it's all I got sometimes.

'Cause I know the way you stare,
pale blue eyes like a machete edge
catching the color of new sky,
the way you barely whisper
your orders, spit out the food,
complain about my shuffling gait,
snorting out my funky smell,
find fault in each task I do,
never right, never good enough,
curse my children like dogs,
'cause I know you just hurting
drooling your bitterness
when my back is turned,
when the shape of my black ass
swings that way you hate,
sashaying through this room of daggers.

I know you're wondering what I've got
down there, in my belly, in my thighs,
make him leave your side,
crawl out of his pale sick skin
and howl like a beast at night,
whimper like a motherless babe
suckling on me, suckling on me.

You can't hide the shame you feel
to know I sometimes turn him back.
I know you know it, from the way
he comes on you hard and hurried,
searching for a hole to weep his soul in —
yes, I turn him back when I want,
and he still comes back for more.
I've got my pride sometimes.

I know the way you try to read me,
try to be me, can't be me,
never be me, never feel the black
of me, never know the blues in me,
'cause you never want to see you
in me even though we bleed together,
finding each other's tidal rhythms,
and bloat together like sisters,
hoarding the waters of the moon together.

So I sashay through your life,
averting the blades with my leather skin.
I abuse you, and when he bawls,
that is my pride at work,
all I've got sometimes.
I'll cook your meals
until he keels over,
and you just have to take it
'cause I took it with no fuss
when he forced his nothing self on me,
while my babies sucked their thumbs
within the sound of my whimpering;
I paid, baby;
I'm just reaping what y'all done sowed.

Dem

Never called a white man *massa,*
never called no white woman *missus,*
just plain old *sir* and *ma'am,*
like I would for any soul who's got
age enough to make me feel like a child.

And just how *daddy* is like *sir,*
how when you speak it you think of God
staring down hard at your body minding
its own business and growing all them hairs
and letting things flow inside of you
making you feel things you never should
and your mouth muttering sin all the while.

Just like that, every time I would
stare at the scraggly grass, dry summer bush
on the edge of the cotton rows,
eyeballing a pebble sitting lonely there
in the sun, just waiting for me to find it
leaning soft against my toes,
under the ragged shadow of our home
looming cool and dark, eating up
the shape of a man on a horse
whose eyes I can't see, 'cause I'm staring
at the way the earth grows dark at dusk.

Just like that, every time I spoke
the word *mister* to boss man Creech,
was like my soul tensing for a crack
of his tongue, like my body saying,
Yes suh, massa, no suh, massa
I will jus' step over yonder and fetch it, massa;

and I could feel his eyes on my head;
could tell he knew the shame of me,
feeling naked there before him and all.

I don't call them nothing no more;
they is just man, woman, dem,
that's all they is, that's all.

Long Memory

And if it is not hate
it must be something
more insidious than hate,
something like the cold
nonchalance with which
small boys slaughter lizards,
must be something
like the casual bloodletting
of livestock at the butchery.

The sheriff does not suspect
hate in the stringing-up
of a nine-year-old, choking him,
beating him — no hate there
in calling him "Little nigger shit!"
No hate in that at all,
just drunken mischief,
for this is the sport of couples
there in Mount Zion
in the dry cold January low country.

How can I explain to you
that I have searched their eyes
and it is still there, the light,
that tells me all this is at the edge
of their precarious lives? How can I
tell you that I still weep
at the news of such cruelty?

My father brought home the news
of a lynched family friend in such
cold whispers that we all mourned

in deepest silence through the night
that closed, inscrutable mantle,
around us. My father stared into
the fading embers of our home fires,
silent as a stone in water.

Fire Makers

In the ragged edge of winter,
the children tested the chill

like naked feet in an unknown pool,
then gathering what warmth

they could muster, they searched
the woods with eyes familiar

with the texture of branches,
and found the dry pieces quickly,

carrying them cradled in their arms.
From the creaking porch,

I watched them return like creatures
birthed among the twisted trunks,

haloed by their rising breaths,
the leaves crackling underfoot.

And always, the flame would fade
only when the last lesson was learned;

before the twilight six-mile trek
to the predictable labors of home.

"How much farther ma'am?"
"Not much farther, child, just beyond the bend."

Gomer's Song

2007

Hinterland

Georgetown, Guyana, 2000

Farther inland, beyond the dank stench
of old soap, shed skin, and spilt piss

in the gangrened gutters, alga-
green in the rich fluorescent way

of rot, elemental rot; beyond the tar-
stained dikes along the indifferent beach,

beyond the stretch of cornfields,
a horizon of green spears scratching

the startling sky, blue, big, so wide,
the hills are small humps undulating

along the bias of the wide
windscreen of this bus. At dusk

the darkness was sudden, the trees
crawling closer to the damp road,

whispering the disquiet of breezes.
So deep inside this land, the twist

of roads, this entanglement of river
and jungle, we arrived at a clearing,

the ground, brilliant white sand
in the moon glow, as if God began

the beach here, then changed his mind,
leaving the shells, dunes, and brittle

sand among the chattering trees,
thick-trunked and wide as houses.

In this place, where the rain came
nightly, thundering on the zinc roof

of the mess hall, we took shelter
under the dripping eaves, and we looked

into the inscrutable dialogue of the night
and poured our stories out, softly, softly.

What We Have Learned

I

We have learned not to keep a tally
of the numbers we make up.

We never share the names we have invented
for who we are: the wounded,
the spoiled, the uncared-for,
the unloved, the broken,
the shattered, the scarred,
the holes, the holes, the holes.

These we keep secret: naming, counting,
calculating the havoc caused
or the weight of hatred we could carry
is more than anyone should bear.

Still we know the story—there is comfort
in the lines we can draw from
this calm capacity to spread ourselves
on floors, broken beds, stained sofas,
filthy yards, battered car seats—
spread ourselves to be taken
surreptitiously in the dark.

How easily we recover to ourselves,
never doubting for a moment
what grace is—we know grace.

All creatures caught in their squalor
know the language of purity;
its gentle hand washing away
the caking of our filth—we know this
well and give thanks for mercies.

II

Our insanities are quiet things.
They arrive in pragmatic calculations,
and we have learned to speak them
in those dark moments when our needs
overwhelm us: *You too will hurt*
me, and I will let you hurt me,
and you will think you have ruled me,
but you will never understand
that I have forgotten the rituals
of hurt — now they come as ordinary
paths to my peace. We have learned
to carry in us the bloom of desire,
a kind of perverse daring that we break
loose in dark rooms, frightening
our lovers with the unfolding
of ourselves. What they won't know
is that each orgasm is a triumph,
each lilting arrival, a prayer
against the rotting of the body;
each little death is a revival,
a kind of sacrament against
the days of such gloom
when we could not fathom
beauty in us, could not turn
our broken bodies into songs,
could not laugh constantly
without the haunting of its ending
looming over us. Our lovers
may not know that sometimes
we shout to deafen the echo
of some lewd urging — something
that belongs to another memory;
that in mid-coitus or in some casual
instance by a tree or a stove,

something spoken can still
in us the ordinary language
of living. We have learned
never to pull the meaning
of our hesitation, our scream,
our sudden freezing into the open.

III

We have learned silence. We know
the story of our unmaking.
We will not tell it easily,
never to explain anything
except the anger that lights
in our heads, making us scratch
our scalps violently; except
the way we can grow distant,
leaving everything behind;
except the loudness of our pleasure,
the way we howl our sweetness.

IV

I will offer only the general facts,
nothing of the detail.
The horror in that is more
than words would allow —
after all, there is a glazed eye
in all of us — some infant child
who has vowed never to speak
again. For her, I too have lost
words. I offer only this:
that my three brothers
and a cluster of friends
raped my ten-year-old body.

Sweet Old Women

A woman wants to sit on the edge of the city
waiting for the young girls to gather at her feet,
to learn the pattern of grass weaved into baskets
or the secret of the sweet aftertaste in the stew —
and she says loudly, *I just stick my foot in and stir,*
which is enough for a day of reverence when age
is a balm over all sins. Just sometimes, one will come
by with tears or the lament of some bruised love
in her — the weight of guilt on her chest, a girl
full of questions about the taste of love, the one
who asks why people don't just fall dead rather
than carry the stone in their chest of love.
Sometimes she sits her down, and they watch
the way the light falls across the street,
the shadows growing long — and in this silence
she chuckles a deep sweetness that grows
into an open-faced laugh, which is wrong
in this time of mourning, but even the girl
must giggle, wiping her face to hide her teeth,
staring back with this question, as if this woman
spread to spilling on her stool has now, at last,
lost her mind.
            But mad women will speak;
old mad women will unfurl the stories they carry
inside them, the stories that have been hiding,
even as they have danced in their heads,
made their skins tingle, made their soft chuckles
bubble out at funerals, at wakes, at the bedside
of some dying soul. Old mad women, if you ask,
will tell you of the secrets they cherish, the men
they have held hostage to their hips in the green
grotto behind the cemetery, the men who wept

to learn of other lovers, the men who crumbled
when their penises remained flaccid, useless,
despite the boasts, the promises, or men who have
turned them into soft flowers, then torn them
petal by petal into the bacchanal of desire, howling,
howling; men who have made them wake late at night
to walk through damp fields smelling out
the hunger of their lusts; and women who touched
them so tenderly, that in their arrivals in those
hidden rooms where women sew frocks,
burn hair, and share the whisperings of the wounds
they have born — there in those menthol-
scented rooms, they felt their skins turned
inside out, their eyes falling deep into gloom,
when they lost the meaning of words
for the first time, for the only time;
when, in the panting nervy heat of the after-
math, they promised never to speak of this,
but always to carry its memory in them;
so that even now, when they think of a name
like Lucy or Merle or Eartha or Una,
they still feel the dew of desire in their vaginas.

Old mad women carry these things and more
in them, and if pushed, if goaded, they will
hum a hymn and then tell of the meaning
of desire. A woman wants to grow old
like such women, the protectors of the gate.
Women who will make even the most wayward
of women understand that the longing
in them, the taste for sweetness on those days
when the blood is gathered deep in them,
is the promise of God, and laughter
is the healing, and memories lengthen days
when they are warm with such thick
pleasures. A woman wants to collect

her secrets so she can have dreams
when the days grow darker and cool.
A woman wants to age like these sweet
old women, copious bosoms full of a hundred
embraces, and laughter wide enough
to ease the broken — women with memories
that do not canker but continue to bloom
into fresher and fresher flowers.

Water Carrier

for my husband, the prophet

I carry water in cupped hands,
I have found a thirsty lip,
I pour, he drinks quickly,
his throat rolling, his eyes grateful.

I dip again, he is waiting,
I feel the soft of his lip
flame my fingertips.

His tongue cleans my palm.
He makes water with his eyes,
beckons me to taste the salt.

I am the water carrier.
I feel the livid sweetness
of my giving, and the bright
alertness of this salt
touching my tongue.

Long Time

...do you, do yah, think about that?

BOB MARLEY

Long time I don't see a morning
electric like a dream what turn out
not to be a dream beat up 'gainst sleep all night,

or a morning fresh like a rhythm guitar
calling in sun is shining with a fat bass
humming righteousness to the soul

like how some poem when you read it first
leave you with salt in your mouth,
frighten you how things ease back.

Long, long time I don't hear a music
could make me think that I don't know,
yet I know how it fit with light.

Want to rub up 'gainst a music,
make it carry me through dew wetness
of Mannings Hill, make me find peace

like logwood burning, the taste
of roast breadfruit and cool slice pear
and a sweet hot cocoa tea.

Impossible Flying

2007

Legend

for Kojovi

A deep-pink face webbed in canary-yellow netting,
swaddled in infant finery — flesh soft to the eye.
This is how we first met; you, unblinking,

a week old, and the order of my life shifted.
I was four and you seemed outside of me,
outside of meaning. The nine months before

were blank, no recollection of waiting
for what must have been our mother's
marvelously round body. For it to turn

to this. At four, I stared at the full-length
mirror, then sprinted to the back of it
to find my revenant. My first inexplicable

equation: the hide-and-seek of my image.
How easily it slipped away. At four,
all was accommodation of mysteries, a new baby

the advent of snails after rain, the wide
valley of guinea-pig grass — a green, fluent sea
on which our cement-and-glass house sailed;

the magic appearance and disappearance
of this man, Neville, our father who grinned
while bearing you like he did gifts

from exotic ports; smiling proudly
with that familiar gap-tooth, his mischievous
eyes gray as a blind man's marble eye;

bearing you, his lump of pink flesh,
eyes tightly shut, fingers curled.
Now the world had changed as worlds must.

Estimated Prophet

...preaching on the burning shore
GRATEFUL DEAD VIA BURNING SPEAR

I am no apostle to this city — but I carry
a gospel in my head. I wear righteousness
like sin forgiven, and on evenings red
and steamy like this, the city a crowding
of sweaty bodies, I cradle prophecies, heavy
truths of God's schemes in my head. On the bus
from Half Way Tree, this healing flame
tingles the tips of my fingers. This old
earth, this old city, this road of sticky
asphalt, this coffin of black people:
O Kingston — no sunlight, no beach music,
just the daily routine of folks hustling a living.

I sit in the heat like a prophet should,
carrying the earth in my brain — the bus
shuddering its way through the dust and exhaust
on Hope Road with the mountains looming
and the road cutting through the plain,
then rising up toward the cool hills.
Tonight, I meet the fear that will haunt me
with faith and the terror of a family
rupturing. In my mind it is a normal day,
and I long to say hello to you, my shadow,
the boy with laughter in each word,
the boy whose eyes are mine. I long
to knuckle your knuckles, laugh at your stories
and walk away with love. But today,
I meet you crumbled against the rusting bell.
You have no name, no language,
just the dull eyes of a stranger.

Impossible Flying

Palms of victory
Deliverance is here!

1980 JAMAICA LABOUR PARTY CAMPAIGN SONG

I

On Kingston's flat worn earth,
everything is hard as glass.
The sun smashes into the city — no breath,
no wind, just the engulfing, asthmatic noonday.

We move with the slow preservation
of people saving their strength
for a harsher time. 1980:
this land has bled — so many betrayals —
and the indiscriminate blooding of hope
has left us quivering, pale,
void, the collapsed possibilities
causing us to limp. We are a country
on the edge of the manic euphoria
of a new decade: Reagan's nodding
grin ripples across the basin's
surface. We dare to dream
that in the spin and tongues of Kapo
perhaps we too will fly this time,
will lift ourselves from the slough
of that dream-maker's decade —
the '70s when we learned things only
before suspected: our capacity for blood,
our ability to walk through a shattered
city, picking our routine way to work
each morning. We are so used now to the ruins,
perhaps more than that, perhaps to wearing
our sackcloth and ash as signs of our
hope, the vanity of survival.

166

In that decade when a locksman
could prance the streets with a silver
magic trail in his wake, how we fought
to be poor, to be sufferers, to say
Looking at you the better one; how
we cultivated our burden-bearing,
white- squall, hungry-belly,
burlap-wearing, Cariba-suited
socialist dream; how reggae
with its staple of faith, fame,
and fortune spoke its revelation
from the speakers of souped-up
BMWs. Gone now, all gone.

We have thrown off that dead skin now;
and the fleets of squat Ladas
are rusting, O Havana.
We've grown too cynical for such austerity
or perhaps we did not suffer enough.
So on such blank and startled days we dream
of flight. How we hope: *Dance!*
Dance, damn it! Dance, damn it! Be happy!
Our apocalypse echoes on the sound system
and we dance. These laws, these new laws,
these palm leaves, these clamoring bells,
so desperate for deliverance,
this insipid green in the future, and we all
stare at the unflinching sky
and will our hearts to fly.

    II

And how you ran, sprinting
down Carlisle Avenue,
your face set against the bare wind;

you were spreading your arms,
undulating in complete faith
in the wind's lift,

the physics of the updraft;
past the low fences,
the skittish yelping dogs,

the streaks of telephone wires,
the hibiscus hedges
a blur of green and pink

and smudged off-white;
and me calling you,
trying hard to bring you back;

me catching up,
behind you now, our heat,
our panting, the slap of bare feet

on the soft asphalt;
and I reached for you,
held you by the waist,

drawing you down;
and it felt in that instant
not like a shattering of faith

but a struggle to keep
you home, for each tendon
of your body throbbed

with the lightness of a body
prepared for flight.
And my betrayal was to become

the burden,
the anchor you had
for years longed to shake off.

Stillness, the gaping crowd
staring at this sudden accident:
two men in a heap

of twisted limbs
on the road;
you saying, *This time, this time,*

this time if you had let me,
it would have happened.
I too felt the vanity

of our beaching.
The bells shimmered;
the dispatches were in:

No one
was flying
no more.

Casting Out Demons

From the cave, a laugh gurgles, surfaces.
You have learned the dialect of my prayers,
a lingo of rules. You laugh, I cast it out;
they are legion; they keep returning.
I came to see you in the daytime, for despite
my faith I fear the terror of night, the way
sudden light plays on my nerves. I imagine your
valley: the gloom, you wondering about
tomorrow: impossible equations. A week
ago, I dragged you from the toilet. I thought
I would find you bleeding. You were only
crying. I reached. You held me, crushing me.

We trained you well. A ball smashed
over the fence and you always were our
emissary, the one to plead. You always were
the tester of waters, the one to ask the old man
for the hard things, to face wrath, to face the gloom
we feared and the blow of denial
with the genius art of tears and the open-
faced plea of the perpetual infant.
He never said no. You think it nothing
now to sail through this, as if
in no time you will come back grinning,
rewarded with the ball in hand.

I pray over your shining forehead.
Your arms are sinew lined; you are
a thinner version of me and not strange enough
for the necessary detachment of strangers.
It is easier to cast out demons
from strangers because I am unfamiliar

with the line separating personalities,
who is to know the demon from the host,
or the evidence of true healing —
a righted mind — in a stranger?
My faith is not tested by the logic
of psychology. It is all spirit and fire.

I mutter my tongues sluggish like the thick
stale air in the room. I am waiting for them
to catch flame, grow wings, to make
your head light, clean, to return you to the boy
who used to laugh with me for hours
over a single image of Roman foot soldiers
swatted by Asterix and Obelix, their sandals
suspended like an empty coil of leather —
the look of comic violence — how we laughed.
The boy is gone. I want to find him,
but you are growing too quickly for him.
To return would be to retard all love — the beard,
the voice, the dropping of fat, the age
in your eyes. Sometimes I see the fear,
as if so far in the recess of your cave,
you are trying to say something,
trying to grant me the faith to believe.

Secrets

So young you learned the entrapment of secrets.
Your history is scattered across the city;
even strangers have seen you stumble, your heartbeat
echoing in your head. They have shown pity
and collected your story; given you food
like alms for the poor. You dignify their pity.
On better days you walk the roads naked;
everyone knows you, knows of you. How easily
you laugh, not stalked by the fear of being revealed.
Who can hold threats over you? *Splashing good!*
you say, laughing, *Splashing good!* You let
it all hang out there. No mystery of your blood
is buried, no sin, no failing, no cheating,
no indiscretion, no embarrassment. It is all
out there, the life without secrets, a superstar's
life. So young, you have learned the tyranny
of discretion, learned to shun it — a simple lesson
I have learned only too late and with pain.
I have lived all turned in on myself, like a poem
trying to see the grace of a mountain's face,
but only caught up in the twisted entanglement
of roots imprisoned in the clay of myth:
my decency, my sanity, the lie of my life.
I am wracked now with the purest envy
for you whose liberty flits windily about you.

Wasps

Road Town, Tortola

I

A tribe of golden wasps has occupied the brightly lit
room with its grand windows looking out into the tiny
fenced-off botanical garden where teenagers grope

at night, school uniforms lifted, crumpled, their hearts
racing at these clandestine acts. This is my mother's
room and we have come to this island, a year after

the quiet ceremony and the sweet assurances
of first marriage, to find something of a cliché
of beach and sun. Fredericton is still frozen

in late April. I have not seen you in years.
You are gaunt, your body taut with casual labor.
So far, you have survived those menial duties.

The voice of Neville, his cultured authority
(a peculiar inheritance), boomed abuse at the white
bastards you had to serve in this tourist nest.

Now you guard a factory with a billy club,
and pragmatic fear (*I tell them take what
they want and I run if needs be. I just make*

alarm — not no superhero. Dem days done.)
You are getting better. Heroics were a symptom,
a kind of euphoric lack of judgment — impossible

strength. Flying in, before seeing you, I worried:
the gap, the ocean, the time, my betrayals,
as if I had planted another wall between us.

These things loom over our meeting,
but we embrace, laughing, almost in tears,
two big men, no more little brother, big brother.

II

Perhaps we can breathe now, I think.
At night, the wasps descend, get tangled
in sheets, and I am stung, sharp and lasting.

We abandon the room for the moonlight
and sweaty air of the veranda — the sound
of the ocean thumping, the occasional light

squall spitting welcome cool drops — the heat,
the frogs, the crickets, the furtive whisper
of lovers in the public garden below.

We make love in the sticky heat, quietly, my arrival
a weight, like all my pleasures when I think of you
sleeping through dreams, my laughter

slipping into tears. I hold her, try to assure
myself that I deserve this, this love, this joy,
while the sting of these wasps pulses in my neck.

Switch

I did not come this time to find you. I came
clouded by my own laments. When I was spoken to,
I stayed dumb — my silence, the deep sorrow
of facing my ugliness, the callous abuse
of misplaced affections. Oh the things I have written!
The blue streak of debauchery I have uttered!

I found you so steady in your remission, I was
envious. I grew impatient at your rituals
of self-pity, but you offered them as a gesture
of love, the familiar code of people who
have learned the ritual roles of blame
and guilt. You were halfhearted at it this time.

We have always known that your
suffering and my assurances are requisite
to this love. This time, seeing me
out-depress you, it may have frightened you,
and it certainly stumped you dumb.

It rained in Kingston that night, quick bursts
that left Molynes Road flooded,
the streets glimmering with the large
pools of collected water. Sunday night,
and Half Way Tree was jumping with brilliant
light and the rapid sound of DJs.

Something has changed: my tender,
beaten-up body, so guilt-wracked,
is a new continent for our love, a foreign land
whose language we are learning to speak.

Mistaken

A man mistook me for you.
He wrote a letter; asked if I was the one
that went berserk at a camp in the hills.

In his remembering, the boy
standing in the mud despite the sudden
glare of an after-rain sky, watching

the other boys, near men, play-acting warriors,
eyes hot with the conviction of such
rituals — screaming their commands,

you defiant, unwilling to play along.
He wrote to me twenty years later as if
he were still the eleven-year-old who never

learned if the silent creature, laughless
and dull-eyed who stumbled from the cage
they kept him in for a night and a day,

was fine, was okay — he wrote as if
he could never shake the clatter
of it all; the sound of a teenager,

his voice just breaking, howling through
the night; the frogs bleating, the wind
crying, the older boys joking, and everyone

forgetting how easily boys become
killers, how easily blood makes men
of us. He said he was glad to see

I was doing so well — such success.
My survival — *your* survival — was his healing.
So when I wrote to say that I was not

who he thought I was; when I said
your mind had unhinged that night,
that your life had stopped for seven years,

that everything stopped growing; when I wanted
him to know of my guilt for not seeing
that someone did this to you; that *they* did this

to you; that it was not weed, not the trauma
of a last child, not envy, not some
diabolic demon, but the brute cruelty

of boys coaxed by pathetic men, so impotent
that they sought to relive their failed
lives in the company of boys;

when I told him all this, he never
wrote back, not once, not again.

Hope's Hospice

2009

Coffee Break

It was Christmastime,
the balloons needed blowing,
and so in the evening
we sat together to blow
balloons and tell jokes,
and the cool air off the hills
made me think of coffee ,
so I said, "Coffee would be nice,"
and he said, "Yes, coffee
would be nice," and smiled
as his thin fingers pulled
the balloons from the plastic bags;
so I went for coffee,
and it takes a few minutes
to make the coffee
and I did not know
if he wanted cow's milk
or condensed milk,
and when I came out
to ask him, he was gone,
just like that, in the time
it took me to think,
cow's milk or condensed;
the balloons sat lightly
on his still lap.

Live Up

for Nichol

How it had me
I couldn't talk.

This what you hear
is like water flow.

How it had me
I couldn't walk.

You might a call me cripple
but this cripple can walk.

How it had me
all I wanted to do

was crawl in a ball
and dead like that,

but see me here now,
see me here now,

man must live, iyah,
man must live.

Making Ends Meet

She sells box juice every day
down by the terminus in Spanish
Town, to make ends meet, get
a little something for school
lunch and bus fare for her
big daughter whose body
is fine like hers, skinny
like breeze could blow her —
tall hair, high bottom, nice
shape. Sometimes it come
in like they are sisters
when they step their way
through the muddy pothole
and marl lanes of Portmore's
dry-back streets, and same way
the men are always asking
for a double mint slam
with two schoolers; and she
knows how to smile, kiss
her teeth and drag her big
daughter along. The girl
now wearing same short
frock and halter top
her mother wears, and mother
know it's a matter of time
before she start show belly,
though she warn her daily,
but girl is girl, and this Jamaica
is a rough place with man
who will lay wait you,
sweet-talk you, offer you
bus fare and food money

each day, and sometimes
he might buy you a nice
shoes—just a matter of time.
And what a mother
who hustling a two cents
selling box juice and icy mint
down by the terminus
in her fade-out denim skirt
and broken-down clog shoes,
with the fabric mangy down
to nothing where her tough
heel must rub every time
she step, can offer to this girl
who start to smell herself,
start to want things?
Fifty dollars for a bag a ice,
the rest is the heat and dust
of the city to make people
thirsty, make them buy.
Ever since she test positive,
nothing won't go right
for her; it come in like
a curse to blight her day—
big woman like this
depend on her mother
for clothes money
for some dollars to buy
pads and panty—what a life!
Man is like a curse on her,
with sweet mouth and lies;
man just take and take,
and all them leave is trouble;
man is like the grave to her,
she see them coming and run.

Yap

He was remembered
his name becoming a common
noun and verb in regular parlance:

A **yap**

yap \ yap \ *n* **yap·pist** \ ya-pest \ **yap** *vi* **yapped** \ yap-t \
[Youthful innovation Jamaica College] (1974) **1:** HOMO-
SEXUAL usually considered obscene **2:** battyman and spe-
cialist in homosexual practices **3:** the scourge of school-
boys **4:** their secret fear when clandestine hands cause
self-inflicted sticky orgasms **5:** something no boy admits
he is to other boys (*archaic*)

A gentle boy with a sharp tongue,
he played chess quickly, aggressively
winning with a laugh — played football

in a torn yellow shirt and red shorts;
his father sold radios and calculators
in an air-conditioned appliance store

somewhere downtown and made good money.
They lured him into the piss-stink toilet
flooded with piss and loose shit,

its blue walls scarred with obscenities —
secrets about teachers, yearnings,
hieroglyphics of a twisted culture.

Nuñez, the short Syrian, was the bait
with his tight pants and benign smile —
securing his heterosexual credentials

despite his lisp and delicate eyes.
And they lured Yap into the toilet
where he thought he'd find a friend.

They beat his head till blood
washed the wet cement floor
and his blue shirt turned purple.

This dizzy day of crows circling,
heating to a haze the old cream buildings,
lonely on the feet-worn dust

under the tamarind tree
sat Yap, wiping the blood
from his broken teeth,

tears streaming, frantic to find words
to explain why he wanted to leave
this school and why his shirt was wet

like that. The Citroën sailed in
and stopped. The door opened, swallowed
Yap. The Citroën sailed out.

Faith

for Nichol, Lorraine, Sherese, Lascelles, Glendon, Tricia, Renesha, Dave, Anneshia, and Paul

Now faith is the substance of things hoped for,
the evidence of things not seen.

HEBREWS 11:1

I

The Seen Things

The news comes like a stone falling.
Suddenly all light is gone.
Outside the heat is black as loss.
Tomorrow is a burden.
I speak the words into the air;
no one answers; the sky
is a dull plate of silences.
Tomorrow is a heavy load.
My feet move sluggishly,
every sound muted to a drone.
It is hard to dream these days,
and oh, the tears, the tears.

This treachery of the blood
is a secret rushing through me
and my face is a mask;
no one must read beyond
its inscrutable dumbness,
no one must know.

I cannot read the faces around me;
everyone seems filled with hope—
how pleasantly ordinary this life

must be for them, I think.
But who can read the secrets we carry
in this city of dust, exhaust,
and the clamor of engines?

II

The Unseen Things

Hope is in the tender hands that hold you.
Hope is in the embrace of the loving.
Hope is in the flesh touching flesh
to remind us of our human selves.
Hope is in the gentle nod of recognition,
hope is in the limping body still pushing
against the pain, the discomfort, still
laughing from so deep down it feels
like the rush of alcohol in the head,
the full abandonment of all fear.
Hope is in the freedom to say
I long to be touched by a lover,
I long to feel the rush of desire
satisfied; hope is to embrace hunger
and find comfort in the sharing of needs.
Hope is in the hands we grasp,
the prayers we whisper,
the amen, the amen, the amen.

III

Evidence and Substance

There is substance in the gathering
of bodies battered by this disease.

There is evidence in the quiet promise
we make to be here again next week.

There is substance in the sweet taste
of coconut water, the scent of morning.

There is evidence in the songs a slim man
sings, as healing as the balm of warmed oil.

There is substance in the expletives shattering
our peace: the tears, the lament, the fear.

There is evidence in the hum of recognition,
the comfort of hands held tightly.

There is substance in the streets walked
to tell people to hope for tomorrow.

There is evidence in the body growing fat
with love, round with hopefulness.

There is substance in the promises we make
to protect this world with the truth of our wounds.

There is evidence in the rituals of the living,
the memories of the lived, the calm we crave.

There is substance in the green of rainy season,
in the harvest of sweet mangoes in November.

There is evidence in these songs we now sing
against the treachery of our blood.

Back of Mount Peace

2010

Found

She did not know her name standing on the hook
of the road to Brown's Town where the chattering ghosts
of forty market women hover. The way she shook,
it was as if she saw them, felt them post
their revelations in her head.
                                   She did not know
her name, this round body, orange in the dew,
when I came upon her.
                                   She was naked, her breasts
low with weight not age, her eyes almost blue,
the negro of her settled in her hips and the curl
of her pubic hair. She shivered on the crest
of the hill, no clues to her life except the thin
line on her wedding finger, a butterfly tattoo
on her sloping shoulder, and the flame-red sheen
of nail polish on her toes.
                                   I asked her who
she was; she said nothing, then repeated, *Who?*

So I named her Esther, and her eyes flew
away from me, high into the sullen sky;
then she sang a hymn that made the pea doves fly.

The Habits of Love

Since his wife Loretta's death, Monty collects
the burn-stained clicking carcasses of bulbs,
storing them in cotton stuffed into plastic
pastel-colored party cups. He shelves

them in the tinderbox-shed in the backyard,
visiting them each week as a ritual
for the dead. He tries not to discard
the multiples, but relishes the collapsed oval

of one he found glowing in an open field,
the sun humming in the shattered filament,
as if the earth fed power to make light bleed
through, so a man would stare in wonderment.

It is still the cherished one, despite the hundreds
he has gathered in the gloomy innards
of his shed. Esther has seen but not said
a thing; so grand his pain, so hard, so hard.

Steamed Fish Supper

She eats the steamed snapper with practiced efficiency
like my mother. She casually sucks in whole parts
then, staring ahead, she moves her mouth, familiarly.

Suddenly, thin white bones make a surreal art
of her lips. They hang there bobbing. She gathers them
into a cupped palm as she swallows the flesh;

her mouth, pink and tender, can now open
for more fish. She knows how she likes it, fresh
and liquid with coconut milk, the bammy steamed

and gummy in the okra slime. Esther does this as if she has
lived in a village where women interrupt their dreams
with the hope of their men returning with bass,

tuna, shark, and pink snapper.
                                    I eat in fear,
praying, hoping she does not remember.

Evidence

She traces with her finger the amber
lines emanating from her navel —
the story of how a body builds layers
of fat to cushion the head of a child

growing in the salt waters swirling
in her. These lines are remnants
of the glorious dome, the swelling
before the release through the crescent

scar under her belly — a keloid
rise that she fingers, a comforting
ritual while she waits at night for the void
of deep sleep. These, plus the evidence

of hard thickening skin just below
her vagina, where the rip of birth
healed into a still-tender furrow
of skin, are the brandings of a mother.

A Woman Wants

She wants a man who can turn his nose to smell rain
before the clouds have come; a man who waits patiently
in open fields for the deluge to soak through his skin.

A man who places his cheeks on her round belly
whispering messages, listening for it to say, *Plant the hoe
now, while I still carry moisture, just below the cracked*

skin of my belly. A man sweats into the land, a slow
laborer whose toes sink deep into soil. He will fall back
to the ground knowing she will cradle him, suck him

down deeply, letting his roots curl around sod and feed
from her constant streams. She wants a man whose eyes brim
with tears at the sight of the first shoots breaking the seed's

shell. This man will know when to be just a breath
and when she longs to inter him in her soft earth.

Sea

Today she stares out to sea, moving her lips
as if she is reading her past in the undulation
of waves, and he watches her, fearful that this will trip
something in her, take her back to the commotion
of her history.
         The sun rests on her. The sea turns red,
then indigo, that deep purple before the black;
and she stares out, silent, waiting.
                  Once, she said
that if it all came back she would lie, pretend the track
back to herself was never there, just so he would
understand that he was her happiness. That promise
seems lost now, with her eyes trying to read
into something on the open sheet of sea, her shoulders
defiant; a back with no assurances, just the dread
reminder that those pleasures, those sweet days are dead.

Seer

Last night
you look

at me hard
then soft

like you see
something

old and sad
in me.

Redux

The road slopes up — wet, it glows blue and white.

The moon will mad you when it catches in the crotch
of the mountain.
                     A woman is standing naked in the light.
We have been here before. A man, his face blotched
with green and silver, tries to will his mind to act,
to do something about this naked woman standing
on the road, her hair slick and soft. Her eyes make a pact
with his — so uncanny the way she turns his seeing
into a merciful blindness; this is a body lost to itself,
and her mind has slipped.
                     You not from here?
he asks calmly. *I don't think so.*
                     The air is deaf
to everything but their breathing. It has been a year
since that first time on the hill. This time she remembers,
and her growing sorrow gives no shelter, drags them under.

Esther's Nightmares

I

The Accident

A hollow house tucked into the shelter of fruit trees,
the neglect is barely showing — there is no life here.

Neighbors approach with averted eyes. They see
their own mortality in the narrative; the bare

windows, the silence. A family's disappearance,
the impossible efficiency of a tragedy that grows

with each telling: the man's body found by chance
by truant children diving in the river's slow

turn near the rocks; the two infants caught
like bloodied tabloid sheets in a tangled mess

of acacia bushes that grow below the rotted
edge of the roads, the tattered magenta dress

of the woman, have all been found. The car's carcass
rusts where river meets sea. We know the rest.

II

The Drowning

She struggles. Her dress ensnared in the submerged
roots of a mangrove tree, her arms flailing
until the red fabric rips; her body fights to emerge
into the cold blue night, after baptism, after shedding
her old skin.
             In this nightmare her man has high
cheekbones, damp horse-eyes and something almost
like despair at the tedium of holding her tight,
firm, restraining her lashing body — so close
to him that she can't pull away before she grows
still, before she fills with river water, before
he is free of her, free to run to the bitch she knows
will hear that it was done quickly, painlessly.

He walks away not knowing that Esther will burst
into fresh air, naked, reborn and full of grace.

III

The First Body

In dreams she imagines a girl's slight body,
her ashy knees touching, her taut belly
a gentle bowl, her braids thick and knotty,
gentle on her shoulders. Her eyes glow
with recognition. She reaches upward
and says, *Mama,* as if these were her first words.

Her calico dress is covered with thick cords
of green vines, obscenely red petals, and a shower
of marigolds. Her arms are thin black twigs,
and she holds herself as if she is afraid to feel
again, afraid to laugh. Above, the red sky promises
nothing but stories that will never heal.

Esther wakes with a stone deep in her belly
and the sadness of a soul missing its first body.

IV

Esther's Daughter Returns

She comes like an old quarrel, her face
red and fierce; her braids wild.
She is a child with too little grace;
then she says, *I hate to die.*

This is a dream. Awake, Esther
knows she can't fight
the resurrection of the terror
of forgotten truths. This light

is harsh, a knife-blade in the flesh,
and she can fight it back no more.
Monty is her peace, the lush
comfort that cradles her.

But Monty is fading into mist.
The ordinary is slipping into hope,
and uncertainty grows a fist
that ruins her peace. She gropes

for meaning, trying her hardest
to beat back the seepage of memory,
knowing that nothing but regret
will come with this resurrected body.

v

Prognosis

When a body surrenders to the truth of its decay,
when the calm truth-telling of a doctor offers
only months and the comfort of pills for the days

when the pain will be too much; the body prefers
forgetting and flight. A woman runs from the rotting
heart of her home, the room where she is waiting

for the cancer to begin to reek; she's sprinting
from the city, from memory, from knowing
herself, leaving the too-early mourners, the plans

for the living that will survive her. She takes a bus
deep into a pitch-black night and then stands

dumbly in the hook of a chilly mountain road
dropping clothing, fear, and every heavy load.

Wheels

2011

The Glory Has Left the Temple

for Gabriel García Márquez

To tell it, I must call it a dream.

A dream on the Caribbean coast of Colombia
where a beautiful black man serves
thick omelets messy with onions and mushrooms
to an assortment of mavericks — dock workers,
professors, maids, three police officers,
five whores, and a clutch of lawyers — at midnight,
sopping up the curdling rum in their bellies
with thick chunks of white doughy bread.

Antonio, the black chef in flowing linen,
has a hand jutting from his belly
to hold hot coals, and above his head
the interlocking, whirling wheels
with shifting eyes blinking back tears
but following our every movement. The earth
has grown weary with too much blood.

Everyone is counting the casualties
like the score of soccer matches.
I could call it a dream, a kind of
Márquezian apocalypse, the memoir
of a novelist being handed the reams
of paper on which he will prophesy
to the wind. Instead, I will admit
the truth: I have been sitting in a hot
room that smells rich with incense
and the sweat of priests who have lost
the language to comfort the bereaved —
priests whose idols have crumbled

to dust. I am listening to the wind,
to the voice in the wind telling me
to write it all down. So I do.

Wise Man

Looking for a god to come from outer space,
So much careless Ethiopians have gone astray

TOOTS AND THE MAYTALS

I long to be the wise man
in the shadows.

Problem is in discernment.

The women wear jewels
and wave veils to trap
us careless Ethiopians,
while the prophets amass
in full makeup
on the television sound stage
to predict with miraculous knowledge
to the viewing millions.

Chances are you will find
among the devout congregation
staring dumbly at the flat screens
at least one with a cancerous toe,
or a foul-mouthed spouse,
or a predilection for porn,
or sharp backache
waiting for the screen
to speak its name,
to speak her pain.

The wise man in the shadows
whispers the end of things
while the world continues
the pattern of beasts

feeding on worms
to be feasts for the worms.

Amen.

Patience

for Sudan

If you wait long enough after the command
and if the rain stays in the mountains
while the sun sucks every shoot from the earth
and the starving crows have scoured
every broken village, every burned-out farmstead,
the searcher of bones can find femurs,
skulls, and the curved vertebrae by the glint
of sunlight on the blanched smooth surface.
There is no need for a nose to sniff out
the sweet sourness of human death —
wait long enough and all tasks become
ordinary, simple rituals of the civil
servant. This is how a nation is cleansed
of its memory, memory of the overcast
dawn filled with the snowfall of ash;
and the shimmering cry of the singer
on the Western Hill, his voice cutting
through the thick gloom, calling all the birds
to a feast of flesh and the intoxication
of blood — that feast that left the courtyards
bare and brilliant by the time of the promenade,
as if all had found themselves ensnared
in the dreams of food and fat cooks
chopping quarter-moons of garlic and rolling
mountains of leavened dough, dreams
of fruit bursting with the perfume
of readiness, as if some seductress has held
them tied to their cots. But the houses
are hollow, the towers have no sentries,
the stones are dark with the sun-drunk
clot of bewildered dogs. This is how

a nation forgets its loss, and hopes for
the impossible of peace come new mornings.
If you wait long enough, all murders
will have lost their scream, all bloodlines
forgotten, all dynamite broken, all storms
settled, all bones cleaned of the memory of sin.

Faithful

> Jah live, children, yeah
>
> BOB MARLEY

I

We, too, will not accept the fictions
arriving from abroad. The emperor,
our precious little man, the incarnate,
the hand of wrath, miracles,
and hope, the surrogate father
for the fatherless and the fathers,
the armor over us, righteous quixotic
slayer of giants, the stone the builders
refused, the conquering lion,
the tiny island that is *tallawah,*
the pebble rushing into Goliath's head,
the grace of Africa, the bearded man
with eyes of eternity, he with many names,
is dead? All messiahs
will walk through their Gethsemane,
face the treachery of Judas,
stir rumors of unlikely death,
but the mystery of conquest over death
is the right of all messiahs.

II

Not even rumors of death
must pass the lips of the dread.
Now we know the lies
of Babylon will know no bounds;
now we know that the descendants
of King James and his diabolic
scribes will continue to debase

all truth; now we know
that the dead must bury
the dead, but Jah liveth
itinually: Jah must live!

III

> If Jah didn't love I
> If I didn't love I
> Would I be around today?
> Would I be around to say...
> MARLEY

Faith multiplies itself
and swells like yeast
in the heat of Kingston.
Our man, our little warrior,
why must they defame you,
why do they try
to confound the prophets?

IV

> ...but I and I know
> dread it shall be dreader dread.
> MARLEY

Here in Kingston the disciples
gather in the upper studio
and wait for the *k'ibat*
of the Holy Ghost which comes
in a simple liturgy of proverbs:
Fools say in their heart,
Rasta your God is dead...
Turn to the alchemy of dub;

make from the detritus
of the poor the golden hope
of reggae; the poor will
believe beyond the rumor.
Rasta liveth; our little man
cyaan dead, our little god.

Rasta

The grand emperor of Harlem
with a Falmouth accent, thick
with raw molasses from the cane
factories, can smell out a legend.
Look to Africa is the prophecy,
and the Ethiope will birth
a hero, no, a messiah. And this Jamaican
Harlem man has read the Solomonic
line, knows the dignity of Abyssinia
and so learns the language of faith,
and speaks it to the broken people
of Harlem. Africa is a land of princes,
Africa is the home of true pomp;
and all is couched in the cadence
of majesty and prophecy.
Despite Waugh with his girlie name
and Oxford colonial stain
going on about barefooted warriors
in their tarnished pomp and ceremony,
or something such, the world understands
the icon of miracles, and the beaten-down
Africans in Kingston's dungle
can dream of a land, so far across the sea,
and an emperor to boot, a black man
with a mane of locks and eyes of steel
and golden scepters — a tamer of lions.
The thick black Harlem emperor
learns that prophecy cannot
be taken back, it will not return void,
and the world will know/ the new skank
to a new rhythm/ and the chant,
Jah, will now be/ followed
by the call, *Rastafari,*
ever living, ever faithful, ever sure.

African Postman

for Solomon Ephraim Woolfe

Son, who is dat?
Is de African Postman, Daddy
BURNING SPEAR

East from Addis Ababa, and then south
deep into the Rift Valley, I can hear the horns
trumpeting over the flat-roofed acacia trees,
see the African women bend low with wood
heavy on their backs, and the cows, goats,
donkeys, mules, sheep, and horses snapped
into obedient herds by sprinting children,
move along the roadside. Life happens here.
I am traveling to the land I have heard about,
Shashamane, the green place, five hundred acres
of Jah's benevolence, and I know now that
I long to hear the rootsman tell me how,
despite rumors of his passing, the natty
keeps on riding, keeps on standing in the fields
of praise to hold on to the faith of roots people.
Brother Solomon, you put the name Ephraim
on your head and carry the face of the true
Rasta, the face of an Ashanti warrior, eyes deep
under heavy lids, and your skin tight as leather,
blacker dan black. I have met you before
on the streets of Kingston, there where you trod
to the hiss and slander of the heathen, you,
natty dread, gathering the people's broken minds
into your calabash. You carry it all, tell them
Return to the roots, the healing shall take place.
You are Burning Spear's voice in the fields of *teff,*
you tell me of the prophecy of Marcus,
and I listen to you, through the phlegm,
through the gruff of your voice, and suddenly

when I ask about the passing of the Emperor,
you rise up like a staff of correction, your voice
reaching back to the mountains, your warrior
self, your yardman greatness, and you speak
a mystery of those who have ears but won't hear,
and those who have eyes and won't see,
and I know/ that this dread will one day stand
in this soil, and find his feet growing roots,
that soon the earth will be darker for the arrival
of Solomon. Let the heathen rage, let the doubters
scoff, let this Ghanaian youth whose eyes
have seen the face of Jesus Christ, let him too
sit and marvel at the faith of the natty.
For this African Postman has forsaken
father and mother, and has come to stand
before His Imperial Majesty, to call only him
Father, so that the Father might call him son,
and the world will carry on its weary march,
and the ibises will swoop in the Ethiopian dusk
and the smoke will rise from wood fires,
and the night will come with news that the rootsman,
after four hundred years of being told
he is homeless, has come home, yes, Jah,
has come home.

> Sons and daughters of His Imperial Majesty Haile Selassie,
> Earth Rightful Ruler, without any apology say:
> This is the time when I and I and I should come home,
> yes, Jah... Nah leggo! Nah leggo! Nah leggo!
>
> WINSTON RODNEY

Reach

I come in search of diadem and scepter.
I come in search of a doddering old man.

I come in search of the glory of warrior kings.
I come in search of the burden of patronage.

I come in search of the eyes that burned.
I come in search of the body in the latrine.

I arrive in a city that has expunged a hero
gone to seed — perhaps he stayed too long
or perhaps he has not gone, not quite yet.

I come in search of the conquering lion.
I come in search of the hubris of empire.

I come in search of the ancient faithful.
I come in search of the blasphemy of Rasta.

I hold in me dusty questioning, seeking
out the whisperers and the scoffers.

It is raining in Addis, the air is thin
and I know only that these faces,
these beautiful faces, are the faces
of those uncertain of majesty.

When man is God and God is man,
myth and magic walk hand in hand
with blood and madness and decay.

In this land, it is possible
to hear the voice of God
in the voice of the dead.

New Poems

Yes, mi fren',
We deh a street again.
Yes, mi fren', mi good fren',
Dem seh we free again...

BOB MARLEY, "DUPPY CONQUEROR"

Steel

A truckload of fresh watermelons,
lemon-green goodness on a slouching
truck, cutting through so many states:
Arkansas, West Virginia, Maryland,
into the smoke-heavy Pennsylvania cities;
from red dirt like a land soaked
in blood to the dark loam of this new
land — from chaos to the orderly
silence of the wolf country — Pittsburgh's
dark uneven skyline, where
we have found shelter
while the crippled leader
waits to promise healing
for a nation starving
on itself. Two men, dusty
from the Parchman Farm,
their eyes still hungry
with dreams, laugh bitter
laughs, carrying the iron
of purpose in them. Hear
the engine clunking, hear
the steel of a new century
creaking. There is blood
in the sky — at dawn, the city
takes them in like a woman.
Inside them all memory
becomes the fiction of survival —
here the dead have hands
that can caress and heal,
hands that can push a living
body into a grave, hold it there,
and the living get to sing it.

This is a nation of young men,
dark with the legacies
of brokenness, men who know
that life is short, that the world
brings blood, that peace
is a night of quiet repose
while the dogs howl in the woods,
men who know the comfort
of steel, cold as mist at dawn,
pure burnished steel.

Dirt

> I got one part of it. Sell them watermelons and get me
> another part. Get Bernice to sell that piano and I'll
> have the third part.
>
> AUGUST WILSON

We who gave, owned nothing,
learned the value of dirt, how
a man or a woman can stand
among the unruly growth,
look far into its limits,
a place of stone and entanglements,
and suddenly understand
the meaning of a name, a deed,
a currency of personhood.
Here, where we have labored
for another man's gain, if it is fine
to own dirt and stone, it is
fine to have a plot where
a body may be planted to rot.
We who have built only
that which others have owned
learn the ritual of trees,
the rites of fruit picked
and eaten, the pleasures
of ownership. We who
have fled with sword
at our backs know the things
they have stolen from us, and we
will walk naked and filthy
into the open field knowing
only that this piece of dirt,
this expanse of nothing,
is the earnest of our faith

in the idea of tomorrow.
We will sell our bones
for a piece of dirt,
we will build new tribes
and plant new seeds
and bury our bones in our dirt.

Talk

No one quarrels here, no one has learned
the yell of discontent — instead, here in Sumter
we learn to grow silent, build a stone
of resolve, learn to nod, learn to close
the flame of shame and anger
in our hearts, learn to petrify it so,
and the more we quiet our ire,
the heavier the stone, this alchemy
of concrete in the vein, the sludge
of affront, until even that will calcify
and the heart, at last, will stop,
unassailable, unmovable, adamant.

Find me a man who will stand
on a blasted hill and shout,
find me a woman who will break
into shouts, who will let loose
a river of lament, find the howl
of the spirit, teach us the tongues
of the angry so that our blood,
my pulse — our hearts flow
with the warm healing of anger.

You, August, have carried in your belly
every song of affront your characters
have spoken, and maybe you waited
too long to howl against the night,
but each evening on some wooden
stage, these men and women
learn to sing songs lost for centuries,
learn the healing of talk, the calming
of quarrel, the music of contention,
and in this cacophonic chorus
we find the ritual of living.

Transaction

Here he comes, dusty worn trousers,
broke-down shoes, cotton shirt
stained with sweat and dirt,
hands big as a house, hands
rough with all the labors
any slave son must do; this man
in a mangy felt hat, with eyes
cool as a coins, here he comes;
call him a sharecropper, call
him the man who could pick
cotton, gin the seed, make somebody
something good; here he comes,
kicking up dust at the crossroads,
singing a raw blues so simple
it sounds like the end of the world;
here he comes, his head full of seeds,
his eyes big enough to see
that a man is a shell if he dies
with nothing to show for it;
but the empty shack of a share-
cropper, a hole to be filled by some other
god's son, at the crossroads,
he will show you two faces,
a smile and a stone; here
he comes, a circle of schemes
in his head; man who knows
that everything has a price,
who knows that even the bench
in the seaside church will fetch
a price for firewood, who knows
that sometimes you have to sell
your song to make a living, sometimes you got to harden

your heart and sell your mama's
dream for a plot of earth;
so here he comes, with a mouth
full of fast talk, and hands,
long and hard, hanging down,
with a big question in his
face: *Tomorrow, after the sweat
and pulse of your hallelujahs
done dried up like morning dew,
what you got to show for it,
eh, what you got to show?*

Apparition

Every story has a carrier, a patron
saint who must haunt every telling
until the story finds an ending.
The man stands in shadow holding
his head, and he is the smell
this woman has tried to forget —
the smell of white folks, the smell
of a boss man who comes around
grinning, says he could use some
stewed okras and corn bread,
and here, so far from the stench
of hog pens and the heavy sweet
of magnolias; here in this cold
city of shelter, she sees him
holding his head, eyes rolled
back like an inexplicable ending
to a story, an ending she is not
prepared for. This woman, her
body hard with labor, an athlete's
body that's aged to bone,
a woman whose regret eats
away at any flesh she may have
collected in her breasts, in her
behind, this bone-hard woman
feels her heart tighten to see
this man, fat, sweaty, holding
his broken head trying to tell her
the end of all stories, and she knows
she has only run from the earth,
but not from the spirit of that
Southern swamp, the memory
of home when everything

cankers. Everything depends
on the brown stone of an old
broken well where they found
him broken, his neck snapped
by the fall while the train
whistled through the woods.

Playing Lymon

All these words, long stretches of phalanxed
words, paragraphs of meandering breathless
speech, everything repeated until one speech
becomes another, and it is hard just to read,
to make out words with the white woman
overseeing it all, presiding, not like the school-
teacher but like the liberal housewife who goes
into the black side of the tracks to round up
dumb-eyed negro boys loitering on the corner,
boys she wants to teach good ways because
she is brave and in the sixties she watched
them walk the gantlet and she regretted
the pursing of her lips and the gathering
of phlegm behind her teeth and the word
nigger climbing over her skin like a blush,
like a shiver, and how now she wants
to make black theater and wants to make
these strapping men say these lines
like a bath; but all that hovers between
the darkened front-row seats and the stage
lit with house lights, is shame – the shame
of a black man who can't read, can't
say the words, whose body feels like
a mountain, clumsily unmovable on stage,
and the too-calm condescension of this
woman also wants to teach him how
to be dumb-ass Lymon, how to be a clown
because she sees clowns and heroes
and not ordinary men; too far away
from books, too long lost from words,
standing there feeling a big heaviness
in his chest and the ghosts of history
around his pulsing body.

Prophet

for Justice Sherman Smith

I and I build your cabin
I and I plant the corn...
BOB MARLEY

When you work to fill another's belly,
the days seem long, the Mississippi sky
wide as hell; as if there is nothing
but this sun dancing over the cotton fields
before you, and God doesn't even sing
in the trees; a man only has his hands,
his sweat, a gut full of crap, and the promise
of another woman's body opening
for him a deep cavern of sweet oblivion
to take him through the night. And no
song will stay long on his lips, no prophecy
can ride him, nothing but the burning
in his feet and the dry routine of a man
living to die. You owe forever, and then
you cough and die. But take a man
on the Yellow Dog, let him feel the speed
of wind on his face, let him know that
the squat cotton groves of Mississippi
farms can leave memory like dreams
will leave at dawn, show him the way
men can build buildings that reach
so high they are like steeples, show him
the roads paved, and the bodies moving
all day and night in coats and cloaks
and with eyes full of going somewhere,
show him the sacrifice of sweat for a little
cash, and that man will one day stand
in the middle of a cold rain, stare into
the sky and say, "God, I am going to build

us a church, and we are going to make
tomorrows in the Church of Steel and Stone."
For here is how a prophet is made,
here is how a man learns the power
of words to make people hope, here
is how a man makes money out of air,
and still can praise the Lord just the same.

Divination

You give them names only after you wake,
after you have studied the patterns of threes —
Shadrach, Meshach, and Abednego in the fire,
but none of these are hoboes, none traveling
from Nazareth to Jerusalem, and not a sheep
in sight, but thieves on the cross, and the noble
Magi have least to say—still you dream these
train hoppers, bleak with hunger, their clothes
loose, ragged, their eyes dancing with mischief
and in the dream you know to follow them
through doors into hallways. You know
to count to three, the third being the closure
of all stories, the arrival at peace. Every
gathering has the loose-legged dancer
with his knobby stick and a mouth full
of lies that rise like moths over the heads
of folks; it has a hand of steel, that engine
soul scowling in the shadows, wanting
everyone to scowl or laugh, and then
the clear-eyed diviner, one eye shut,
the other reading that pattern of clouds —
every gathering has a sermonizer to balm
the faithful, has a rod to beat against
the stone, to frighten the wolves in the gloom;
every meeting place has its anchors,
and the believers will come softly.

Revolution Man

Old Ishmael talks with the auctioneer's speed —
he knows to take breaths mid-sentence,
to turn every period into an ellipsis; to master
the conjunctions; a chain so unbreakable
the interviewer can only grunt and wait
for the diatribe to end, which it won't
because he's a preacher and there is never
enough time for the preacher who will
start at Stono with its live oaks bearded
by the moss of humid climates, each
aborted dream, all the stolen stories
those white folks collected when "negro"
was slave and the secret of our genius
was best kept quiet in polite company,
all the way to today when despite his good
salary and the acres he has tended even
there in Mississippi, he seems to know
that something, a whole damned lot,
is due him; and this is how a man
makes something of himself, how
a race-man is born, how a man prefers
the chaos of boogie-woogie
to the familiar lament of the blues,
how the radio is his sword
and the poor interviewer can only say
"thank you," as though something was stolen
from him. But out in the street,
out there in the August heat, the Berkeley
streets smelling of dog-mess, he is just
a red-skinned old negro shuffling
his way into the revolution he made,
danced in, and then saw leaving
his body as heat leaves the body.

Traveling Man

And if we cannot take to the road,
wandering away from the ordinary,
leaving behind those who wait
with bitterness and dreams, those
who must invent hearts for us,
must make poems of our voices, those
with nothing but an old shirt,
some broken-down shoes, and a stained
handkerchief left behind to say
a man lived here; a man's body
filled these rooms, to make our
shadow fall on all suitors,
all surrogate fathers, a shadow
that makes them listen late
at night for the click of the lock,
makes them wonder when they will
be found out, their bodies restless
in our beds; men who constantly
wonder at the quiet resignation
in our women; the unstated truth
that if we come trudging our way
back through the dusty town,
turn around the corner, push
open the gate and stand on the porch
looking out like we have never
left, they will take us back
with careless indifference, hiding
the homecoming beneath corn bread,
bacon chunks and beans, soggy
greens to tell us that home is a constant
distraction, that everything changes —
if we can't journey like those
Wining Boys, those restless journeymen,

we learn to transport ourselves
in dreams, long rugged dreams;
that when we wake our faces
are set like those strangers', our
hands and feet have forgotten
the routine of our day to day; and
in those moments, on the porch,
waiting for it to return; we know
the heart of traveling, the exquisite
healing of occasional flight.

Penitentiary

On another stretch of your journey, say along the
Mississippi River Delta, you see rows of black
prisoners chained together working in fields
under the careful vigil of armed overseers. At first
you wonder, has slavery really been abolished in
the South? But your guide assures you that these
are *convicts* on the chain gangs, not slaves.

MARK COLVIN, *PENITENTIARIES,*
REFORMATORIES, AND CHAIN GANGS

It is not like summer camp, nothing so mundane,
it is the hut in the wilderness among the bramble
and acacia bushes, the flat-headed baobab, stingy
with its shade, it is the haunt of dust-covered mangy
creatures, the stench of tooth and claw, it is the path
of stone and thorns, the shame-old-lady, a dull
green shrub closing its leaves to the touch of a foot
misplaced, it is the alertness and caution of prickles
and hardened earth, it is the sun relentless in the sky,
it is the freemasonry of water-finders, the secrets
of rainmakers; it is the bony shoulders of pot-
bellied babies, scratching their arms, staring at you,
their skins white with caked mud, their knowing
seeing, it is the way the sun sets red over the land,
the lines of red dirt climbing toward the clouds,
it is the slow shuffle of a coffle of men, in single
file, their heads shaved to a gleam, their eyes
red with the daze of chewed leaves, their arms
swinging, bodies bare in the setting sun—these
men, still boys, coming so far out in the wilderness,
nervous at the growl of creatures in the shadow—
it is the place where their foreskins will be shed,
where they will learn the efficiency of knives,
where blood will be spilled and sipped, where

they will hear the shattering of screams
and see the dark lines of the griots, arms waving
against the fire, where they will know nothing
and everything, where they will learn the names
of their brothers, the warm voices
of their brothers, the lament of their brothers;
it is here in this barren place where all music
comes as a croak at first then tastes like God
in the wind; it is like this, like this, this ritual
march into the belly of the beast, and we know
that only some return whole, only some return
at all; that only some imagine this as other than
it should be. Our men are in search of the primordial
rituals of maturation, and find it in the bastardized
edifices of their undoing, of the parchment.

Piano and the Drunken Wake

She will not touch the piano, not since
the hallway emptied of those who came
to say the things people say; those who
could tell already the slow-
dragging drinking here, the kind mourners
do, the kind that makes women sit tilted
in the shadows and just weep as if
they don't even know why they are weeping,
the kind that weighs heavy on people,
the kind that leaves plates of fried
chicken to grow hard on the table,
the kind that makes men sing the hymns
they haven't sung since they were boys,
the kind of drinking that don't laugh,
that don't cause commotion, that make
a full room seem like the party was over
half an hour ago, the kind that made sister
Melba wet herself while sitting
on the upright chair for her back—
and she didn't move, just let
the whiskey-stewed piss settle
under her and raise its own
sour stink in the room—the kind
of drunk that made it all seem
like people are underwater; even
though this was a drinking time
not seen in such a long time, they
say; heavens, us having a good old
stomp and grind to see that big-
headed man arrive with his two
long arms and little else to show.
Since then, she has not touched

the piano, left it there as a
witness, as atonement, as that
millstone around this whole
house, dragging them down;
and to this day, the room is
unsettled with stubborn folks
who will not leave until
the lady sings.

Playing Wining Boy

> Maybe this is true. That there are some of us
> who give love and some of us who take love;
> and that those who give can't help giving just
> as those who take can't help taking; and maybe
> this is what holds the world in balance.
>
> CHRIS ABANI, *SONG FOR NIGHT*

The fat man is shrinking at night;
he strips to stare at the melting of flesh,
and his beard grows as if it is sucking
nutrients from his body, the long
gleaming strands coil and dance on his
face — he counts the rivulets of veins
on his arms and he feels the weight
of indulgence lifted — now his trousers
are falling off his waist; he enters
the wardrobe like this, a man half
his former self to be fitted for a haggard
part, a blues piano man with dusty
shoes and gleaming black suit
and a mouthful of dreams.

The fat man is learning the secrets
of women; he is not as old as the piano
player and has not learned the dialect
of taking gifts offered with quiet
disregard; the fat man knows he has
been so soft that hot days make
him weep for the bodies overheating
in ticking projects, and in his fantasies
women mount him, beat his face,
spit on him while riding out
the brute orgasm telling him to say
"love," or "sugar," or "mango" or some

such concoction; and he sings
for them as they bruise him
with the burn of rough pubic hair.

The fat man stands under the lights,
lets the piano man mount him,
lets a blues catch his powdered
beard aflame, the fat man is harder
now, leaner, hungry, and his eyes
squint with the grimace of need.
They will applaud the fat man,
let him take expansive bows,
shower him with accolades,
wonder if he remembers
how easy it was to be
insulated by fat and flesh.

Elevator

You learn faith in that elevator,
faith and service; learn how to believe,
learn how to make others believe,
learn how to take people where they must go,
where they are scared to go, away from
where they have been; you learn to
be the guide, the prophet, you teach
them the constancy of God, you press
a button, call out a number and it will
climb, all the way up—here you learn
how to fly in the house, you reach
into the heavenly places, above it all,
and you are Lord of your kingdom,
here where you can pray, so close,
so close, as close to a mountaintop;
and it isn't hard to hear the pain
of people, see the bruises in a face,
listen to the lament of those who want
to fly some other way. Since
the market crashed, since Roosevelt
come out like a grandaddy
and tell people to hold on, tell
them how he's got something
for you, you've seen how shiny
a white man's suit can get, how
black his collar, how worn
down the heels of them women
with their stockings painted
to hide the holes—or no
stockings—can get and you feel like
the angel in the architecture
riding up and down, and you

know that this is why a man
must turn to God, build
a church, know that this is just
the cage where a bird will sing;
for you know how riding this
box to heaven and then down
to hell could teach you what
it feels like for the Holy Ghost
to light your head aflame, and you
know you want your sanctuary
there in the neighborhood, to be a box
taking folks as high as they can go;
know at least there you can say
you own this, you own this,
'cause you built it with your own
two hands. This is the salvation
of the preachers in this land of beasts
who want to own you, own
everything you have, own
the sweetness of every orgasm
you howl, own the clock
of your broken body, own
your hallelujahs and your amens;
and all you want to do is let
your people own you, let them
shelter you, so you can give
them the guiding, be the elevator
man running them up to higher
places, to the mountaintop,
to the open sky, way above
the city of hands scarred
with the accidents of labor,
this stretch of concrete
and cold, where a soul could
lose itself, where a woman
could slowly dry away to nothing,

where she can forget the hymns
in the rafters, the oil on hands
laid gently on her, the grounding
of soil, the truth of herself,
the succor of tears — a man
knows the call of God to make
him the preacher of faith;
just hold on, Hallelujah,
just hold on, Amen;
just hold on, we going up!

Avery

Fling me the stone
that will confound the void

KAMAU BRATHWAITE

The plague of messiahs arrives thirty
years into this pathological century,
and the apostate scribes have
turned each crisis of faith into
a punch line. In Trinidad, Man-Man
complains about the fool who tosses
too large a stone while he hangs on
the cross; so we laugh as he, like
Bedward, the wingless flier, is taken
away, like that Jesus man
on Guyana's wild coast whose
demise is not so funny, not really,
because we knew that these
Holy Ghost–God men have spoken
an ital truth shattering the myth
of the auburn-haired Jesus
with his stoic chin and Aryan
eyes. These Garvey men, these Howells,
these John the Baptists, these Averys
are making the hearts of the poor
black folk fill with something
holy: full of belief in the comeliness
of black-skinned folks and their hands.
Africa is paradise, and priests
and kings live inside our skins.
It is not so funny when a man
spits on the lies of those missionaries
of our denigrations, not so funny
to think of the women sitting

alone in the makeshift chapel
of captured zinc walls and rough-hewn
benches: an altar of boxes
and carefully nurtured plants
in cheese pans, the women there
at dawn, their faces full of questions,
wondering what is next
while their prophets have been
taken into the asylum, kept
for good, wondering how faith
is made in the face of such
loss — not so funny to know
that in 1936, the anointing
of prophecy has been upon
ordinary men, or ordinary women,
ordinary black folk and the world
could not comprehend it — these stories
hurled to confound the void.

A Good Woman Blues

O Lord, Berta, Berta, O Lord, gal oh-ah,
O Lord, Berta, Berta, O Lord, gal well.
Go 'head marry, don't you wait on me oh-ah,
Go 'head marry, don't you wait on me well.
Might not want you when I go free oh-ah,
Might not want you when I go free well.

LEROY MILLER AND A GROUP OF PRISONERS

When you are out on the road, hustling
shelter in some taking-woman's hovel,
when you wonder how long you will be
a broke bluesman with only some
twenty-year-old story of how you were
somebody, how you sat in the same
studio where big-ass Ma Rainey
used to sit and drink bourbon; of how
people knew you, knew your voice,
how it was to buy a suit, walk
the country street and hear your
voice on the radio, and it has been
so long these stories like your clothes
have gotten so thin they don't keep
you warm no more; and when out
there, you walking to the crossroads
where you meet all kinds of monsters
and ghouls and where you learn
how to limp and use your big
stick to part the arms of women,
you have nothing to keep you going
on dark nights when everything
feel like crap, and you are fifty
years old and you are not dead
and you have nothing to show for it;
no child who ever called you daddy

'cause you never stayed long enough
for them to smell your skin,
for you to hear them say it;
and you know that going back,
you will spoil all the lies
those women told for you, about
their daddy who will walk
around with his big hands
as his only instrument; who can
make a woman take off
all her clothes on the spot
and leave her man just by
the weeping and lonesome
feelings he can make with the piano.
That sharp-faced, cool-eyed man,
their daddy, who took a schooner
to France where everybody knows
his name — if you go back
with your tired self, looking
for a nip of booze to keep you warm,
and some fried chicken
for old times' sake, what good
will that do? So all you have
is this one truth: that Cleo
is your Penelope and until
they nailed down that coffin,
she stayed the one good thing
you ever did; she was a good
woman and she loved you,
and sometimes that is all a man
needs to keep on walking,
sometimes it's all a man's got;
all that has kept him from
the chain gang to the juke joint,
along those lonely roads
cutting across America —

that Cleo is all he ever had,
and Lord knows, she waited,
but you can't outwait God,
Lord, Berta, Berta, you can't
outwait the Lord.

Soldier Man

Sometimes the sound of English coming
out of a man's face, the way it settles
on you like a welcome, even if it is
the English you heard, laced with
tobacco and old cotton money, the English
with burrs at the edge, the sharp
whine so close to that rebel yell;
a sound that makes the hair in your
armpit prick you; even then, here
in this blasted country where death still seeps through the smell
of mown grass, diesel, and acrid
gunpowder, through the cold,
their language comes at you like
a muffler over all things; right in
that moment when you know
they are calling you dog-mess
and worse; you understand America
as if suddenly you belong somewhere,
can say to a man, "So where you
from?" and he will say, "Oxford,"
and you will know the paved road
into that town and the way
rain sets over the trees in October,
and the smell of a smoking hog,
and the sound of a bluesman
still picking on his guitar and stomping
his foot despite the dead droop
of the left side of his face where
a two-by-four settled all smiling;
and he still nod to the white folk
who love to hear him pick
and sing the meaning of home

into the air — here in this country
of mud, white pussy, and death,
you have your gun, you have
your boots, you got your cigarettes,
and you know the taste of killing,
how the world don't stop when
a white man takes a bullet
in the neck and bleeds like anybody
else, and bleeds like anybody
else, and dies; and nobody even
thinks, "Nigger, what you doing?"
Here you understand your only
nation, you have no choice,
you are either nothing or a damned
nation, and you salute that flag,
call the cracker your brother,
and march on, damn it, march on!

Rupture

All about me the ruins of marriages — I have
started to count the long list of familiar
patterns; the women quietly planning
their escape, dead-eyed. They have long
stopped crying — how tender the sound,
how easily Gladys explains her lovers —
it was never sordid, this addiction, and
the sins of her man are the issue after
all; or Paulette her secret of desire
he does not know, he just fears and
she too plots the economy of rupture;
and Gloria is losing weight, sweating
out the summer after her months of
pleading for his touch — now she no
longer needs his touch, she has her
fingers and the consuming pleasure
of plotting her departure —
and these men do not know, all they know
is the cold draft in the middle
of the bed, the quiet compliance; and
they are delusional for they have
no language for this. My friends
are falling away — at forty-five
I have counted fifteen dismantled
marriages and there is now over me
a shadow as if to hope in tomorrow
is vanity — I live each day waiting
for the stomach's collapse when she
will declare me another of the long
line of hopeless men, when we, too,
will know the dry brittle air of disquiet —
hope to imagine happy. The absence

of shadows, storms looming, the clay
when each evening of laughter
does not feel like ominous calm
before the shattering of all things.

Coreen

For all the Coreens, the women who know
that *pretty* won't be said around them; who
know how it is to be with pretty, and pretty
draws a strange kind of tongue-tied attention
from men; they know how pretty can laugh
like pretty does not know that these men
feel too small, too ordinary for them; they know
that pretty doesn't have to make sense,
that pretty usually can't turn a man's
eyes in his head, that pretty wouldn't
know the first thing about the sweet
tumbling in the stomach; they know
that pretty has lived with a key
to the world with her pretty skin and fine
hair and thin wrists, and they have
stood beside pretty and seen how men
look through them to see pretty. You,
all the Coreens, who know how to
look at a man and make him know
that there is a whole lot of woman
there, that in the dark, when he's
holding on to her and weeping
like a baby, that she can teach
him the meaning of woman; for all
the Coreens who wait around
for the men to get sick of pretty
and her skinny self, and who came
to them because they know how to make
a man understand himself, and they
can teach a man how a woman thinks,
and they got all the juice to give
to him making him sweetly drunk

with her with the red sun falling
behind the city blocks; for all
the Coreens who have taken it all in,
and have come out of it with their
heads high and a deep pragmatic
song in their chest, I bow, offer
thanks and grant you nuff respec.

Prophet Man

We prophesy every day; put words out
in the thick muggy air, and they come
back to us with something else —
you have to know that it is not chance
but the poetry of drama when two
players are talking and just when
they speak the name of another
in the air, just when they lay
the path for him to come, he walks
up smiling so they can say, "Man,
you will live long — I was just
talking about you, and look,
there you are." And some people
want to call it chance, like they
don't know that a traveling man,
a man with many addresses — four
or five — a man who is always
coming and going, that man is
a conjure man who wakes up
every morning, listens to the wind
or the sound of the city, or the hush
of trees, and says to himself,
"Where do I go today?" and he goes,
and when he gets there, it is always
the same 'cause people never
expect him and yet they are always
expecting him, and even when they think
they are not, when he gets there, they
know they have been waiting for him
ever since he left his scent in the air
and walked away leaving them
missing something. This man

has a clock in his head that tells
him how long a body needs to miss
him to welcome him with joy;
knows when he's been one place
too long, long before anybody
knows they getting sick of him,
knows how to enter a drama
at the right time and how to leave;
knows when he will find gifts,
and when a cut eye is all he will
get. He is a magic man, a reader
of signs, and nothing is an accident
with him, 'cause when you see
him, you want to see him,
when you hear him, you need
to hear him, and when he's gone,
he's always coming back.

The Actors' Meeting

When the white folks were gone,
and we the talent could gather in the dark
community hall, late at night,
to talk about the play,
the conjure man chuckled and said,
"Don't you know what that man
is putting in your mouth? Don't you
know that the Yellow Dog is some
Klan in reverse; setting things right
that was wrong in the middle
of *Gone with the Wind?* Don't you
know that everybody on that stage
is lying, that they all know who
has been killing white folks
in that Mississippi county, and there
they are acting it all out
like we are talking about ghosts,
and spooks; don't you know
that conjure man trickster, August
Wilson, is throwing words at
all the white folks he knows
are sitting there watching this play;
that they are laughing and weeping
and feeling better than each
soul on that stage who is just
a straight killer — a revolutionary
that shed the blood of white
folks with blood on their hands?
Don't you know that even
this nice white lady director doesn't
have a clue that this play is about
the rightness of vengeance

and the dream that negroes will stop
killing each other and kill those who
need killing? Don't you know
that is what you are playing
on that stage? You couldn't know,
'cause if you did, you would stop
behaving like some damned
plantation slave begging for that white
woman's approval every time you
open your mouth; that is what
I am saying." And they all just
look back at him, and he could
see in their smile that he is just
seeing something they have seen
long before this drama came to them,
and the Yellow Dog is whistling
down there in Sumter County
where the scar of train lines
have been dividing the world into
Manning Avenue and Liberty Street.

Salesman

Here comes the man in his dusty car,
he's got bad teeth but he loves to smile.
He's not a noise maker, he moves quiet
and always looking nervous. He won't
argue with anyone, he just seems to
arrive right on time, when somebody's
lost a job and the rent man is waiting;
or a man's been told that the girl
he has been messing with is pregnant
and looking to talk; or a church
has just split up and the pastor
is looking to rent a new hall for
his living; or someone has just
gotten off the train three days now,
and the dream and the change he has
is drying up fast; or a woman just
had a fight with her daddy and is
on the street with what little she
has; but he always knows when
to come with a soft voice asking
people what they have. He always
finds his way to bars, sits
there nursing a whiskey and tapping
his foot to the music, and he will
always buy the guitarist something,
or maybe the drummer or the piano
player, and he will come every night—
a white man among black people—
and he will wait because sometimes,
somehow, the blues will be real
for somebody and he will simply
say, "What you got?" This man doesn't

buy clothes, won't buy a radio
from you, not even jewelry —
all he wants is that thing you have
to make music. He will take it, pay
you clean money, shake your hand,
asks no questions — an old piano you've
lugged all the way up from the South
that doesn't play right; a rusty
harmonica, a stringless fiddle,
an old guitar, a tambourine, heck, a church
full of tambourines; a pennywhistle,
a saxophone, a horn full of spit,
a snare or two, some chunks of wood
a guy likes to knock together, a bucket —
just anything that can make music,
keep a rhythm, make folks jump up
and dance — he will take it off you;
and if he could, he would buy your voice,
push it down in his sock, and walk away
with it still humming with years of song
through the darkest night.

Creed

Berniece don't believe in nothing. She just think she
believe. She believe in anything if it's convenient for
her to believe.

AUGUST WILSON

She knows what comes with believing in God:
then you have to believe he is not a kind
God, and you have to believe he hates black
folk, and you must believe he could have
stopped Crawley from going out that night
to get shot by those white people over some
firewood — that's what comes from believing
in God. You believe in God and you wonder
who is listening to you at night when
you let a man move on you, and then
you know he won't be back; you believe
in God, you will hope he comes back
and you will be disappointed always
because he won't be back, he never
comes back and where is God then?

She knows what comes from believing in ghosts
or spirits walking the path. If she does,
then she has to wonder if that smell
of her husband's sweat late at night
is him coming by to stay with her, and
then she has to wonder why he never comes
when she needs him; she will have to wonder
what all those old folks and younger boys
who had to eat their own dicks while
hanging from a tree with these crackers
looking on, what are they singing now?
How can anyone believe they can hear those

voices? What kind of noise would that be?
She knows what comes from believing in
the rumors of trains filled with the lost
souls roaming around with the hunger
for vengeance; if you think this, if you
carry this, you can't go on, you can't
live like the world is in what you can
carry in your hands, what you do with
your back, how you make things happen
on your own; how nothing is given
to you and nothing is taken from you.

She knows why she can't believe in nothing,
why she can't believe in prayer, 'cause
praying is to weep, praying is to beg,
praying is to throw your hard body
against the night because you have
nothing else; music is a lie, music
will make you soft, will take you
away from the things you can hold
in your hands; music, those songs, that
sound will wash you, make you fall
apart with nowhere to go. No, a woman
must believe in nothing, and nothing
will take her in. This is how you make
your world small enough for you
to wake up each morning and breathe.

The Transaction

Miss Ophelia with the watery eyes
was well cared for by her lanky
big-bellied husband, Sutter, who would
look at her laid out in white
on their bed and think what a sin
it must be for him to mount her
and do with her what he would
night after night on the road
back from the grounds in the string
of huts smelling of stale collard
greens and the raw smell of slaves,
the smell of the woman who gave
him milk, the smell that makes
him hungry and small and horny
all at the same time. But for
Ophelia, with her watery eyes,
he sees only the parchment
of her skin and feels only the need
to cover her, keep her as pure
as she first was — his nightmare
is to see Boy Willie, the strapping
African, pushing into her, like
a dog would into a bitch —
he wakes up sweating hard,
and sleeps only after some rum.
So come each anniversary
he will find something grand
for her. The girl slave Berniece
or the pony she loved so much,
or the French perfume he bought
in Mobile or the Chinese fan
a traveling huckster sold to him

for some produce and his last coins;
but this time, he wants her to have
a gift of pure beauty; so he will
sell to Nolander, from Georgia,
a slave and a half for a piano,
which is how folks lived then;
how a slave could be here one day
in the bosom of family, right
beside the old live oak tree where
the afterbirth and umbilicus
was buried and the next day: gone
where the soil smells different;
where folks talk and eat different,
and where you can't read the sky for rain.
But he got the plans, and old
Berniece, the matriarch, and that small
boy, Papa Charles, were gone,
uprooted, taken away, just bring
some music to Miss Ophelia; ah
the currency in this instruction — blood
in that piano, everything in that piano,
and she plays it day and night,
while he plants his seed in brown soil.

Thieving

When does the debt end? How long must pass
to make up for your hundred years of taking
from people everything they have and giving
nothing in return? When is the debt
full-paid? How much thieving and
killing must a man do before it turns
into sin, when all he is doing is taking
back what was taken from him, from
his father, from his father's father?
How many bales of cotton must a man
steal to make up for all the cotton
he picked that went into somebody
else's pocket, somebody else's belly?
How many stacks of wood can you
take before you have covered
all the losses; before you have
repaid what a man has done
to that pink private place
of your mother's mother, that thing
that left her covered in shame
for the rest of her life; how many
pianos can you steal for the
bones in the backwoods, for
the anthem of those leading
us to the blackened bloated bodies
of those boys whom they lynched
at midnight under flambeau light—
how much thieving can a body do
before it balances things out? How
much can you take to feed the gap
in a people's memory, the erasure
of the language of the ancestors,

the deafness they caused you
to the whisper of the gods; the house
of bones, the valley of bones,
the deep rift valley of bones,
covered by the weight of the Atlantic,
where the water stripped these bodies
of all their flesh, all they had
in the bowels of their undoing?
How much does a man have to steal
before he can say, "Now I have
all they took, now all I am getting
is what they got fair and square;
now we are even; now I have
what is mine, and every time
I take from them from now on,
you can call it thieving"?

Four Songs for Berniece

I

If she hits him, his arms dangling,
makes a fist and pounds his chest
or his shoulders with her open palm reaching
for his face—like she wants to test
him, to see whether he will flinch, whether he will
cry out his guilt—if she lets the tears
fall, bawling out expletives in a shrill
voice she never knew was there
in the pit of her belly, then maybe,
afterward, her arms aching, her skin
slick with exertion, some sweet mercy
will fall on her, and the man: her man
whom they took from her — stole from her —
might rest at last in peace forever.

II

All she knows are men, generations
of men who come and go, leave you
wondering if in God's creation
there is a place called the blues
where they go to find their hearts,
to find the things someone stole
from them; where they might chart
the patterns of their tired old
stories, where maybe a tender
hand will heal them, send them back
home to stay, to surrender
to love's promise. But life has a knack
of dragging them out again,
leaving her waiting, waiting, waiting.

III

After a while you turn the bitter taste
of loneliness into something sweet. A manless
home can be filled with a woman's praise song
to Jesus—and know that holiness
can be sweeter than a man's body close
to you; and you can go when you want
to go, come in, don't have to find his clothes
in the corner, don't have to sit and count
the hours he is gone; and you know
he has women so why pretend? You are free
of guilt or jealousy; you learn to grow
a tough callus against the enemy
of your flesh; and sometimes, Jesus,
you learn the weightlessness of loss.

IV

Maretha, never be ignorant of men:
you got uncles, you got blood, your daddy's
dead for being a man; their burden
isn't your burden; all you've got is charity,
the Bible says, and good sense to know
that you will love men and they will
hurt you, and make you grow
big with the power of survival.
Some sweet day, the hurting will leave
their blood, washed out by time,
but until then you must cleave
lightly, don't let them entwine
you and drag you down deep;
you've got to stay afloat, got to keep.

If You Know Her

If you know your woman, know her rhythms,
know her ways, if you paying attention
to her all these years, you will know
how she comes and goes, how she slips
away even though she is standing in
the same place, you will know that her
world is drifting softly from you; and she
may not mean it, because all it is
is she is scared to be everything, scared
to be finding herself in you every time,
scared that one day she will ask herself,
all forty-plenty years of her, where
she's been; if you know your woman,
you will know that mostly she will
come back, but sometimes, when she
drifts like this, something can make her
slip—and then coming back is hard.
If you know your woman, you can
tell by the way she puts on heels,
and she does not sashay for you
because it is not about you — how
she will buy some leather boots
and not say a word about it,
and you only see them when she walks
in one night, and she says she's had
them forever; you will see the way
she loses the weight and pretend
it's nothing, but when she isn't seeing you
looking, you can see how she faces the mirror,
lifts her chest to catch a profile,
and how she casually looks at her
ass for signs of life. If you know

your woman, when you are gone she
will find things to do, like walk
alone, go see a movie, find a park,
collect her secrets; and you won't know,
because she is looking for herself.
And she won't tell you that she wants
to hear what idle men say when she
walks by them, because what you say
is not enough. If you know your
woman, you know when she's going
away and you will feel the big
hole of your love, and you can't
tell why she's listening and humming
to tunes you did not know she heard
before, and she will laugh softly
at nothing at all. If you know your
woman, you will see how she comes
and goes, and all you can do is wait
and pray she will come back to you,
because you know that your sins
are enough for her to leave and not return.

Role Playing

Late at night, after the slow farewells
in the dusty parking lot of Patriot Hall,
and you still have the rough stiffness
of whitening on your beard and hair;
and your heart is still humming from
the orgy of applause, the delight
of remembering all your lines; and your
clothes: ordinary trousers, sneakers,
and T-shirt still smell of the stage,
the sweat on your skin from the heat
of the lamps, and inside your head
he is still there, that music man,
the trickster, that fellow always
looking for a dollar, who can
smell money like a fly can smell
crap, and who gets all abuzz
with fresh life when he sees
a dollar he can have, that man
full of stories, whose conscience
is so cold to the tears of women —
it is the way things are — who sleeps
easy at night, does not even
know the chemistry of sin
and redemption: the man
you want to be sometimes —
that man who took a man's
woman, had his pleasures
with her because he knew she would
be thankful for the fifty dollars
he gave to get her husband less
time in jail — and he is now
smiling at that man's son,

and saying cool as can be:
"That was one bad lucky nigger,"
that man you have met
on the tube in London, mellow
with beer and an easy way
with tales; or at the bus stop
in Kingston waiting to head
down to Mountain View Avenue
with a fare, eyeing the women
going by — that ordinary man
of appetites, and you ride
through the dark streets of Sumter,
Paul Simon singing, "Bonedigger,
bonedigger / Dogs in the moonlight..."
feeling him rising into the hot July
air. And when you get home,
you stare at the lines in your face
in the mirror, the gray in your hair,
and laugh his belly laugh
before you shower
what is left of him off
your body one more time.

The Host of Holy Witnesses

I

for Frederick Douglass

To think right there where Booth stood, a squat
negro in a suit is talking about the rights
of white folk and the law that they've got
tied up with their rights; imagine tonight,
a stage full of ordinary black people
looking like my slavey family, turning
our heads aflame over a piano's simple
music, and I can tell the spirits rising
are old as dirt, old as my skin, and my heart
swells to know that these white folks
will see how we have come so far,
how we can call on ghosts to choke
the beasts that held us back so long,
Lord, we come through, so bold, so strong!

II

for Harriet Tubman

August, you are red like some white man's
bastard, like one of those negroes who would
never leave with me because your chance
for a good life was best where you stood;
but, Lord, you know yourself, and how you know
the voice of those spirits that used to talk
to me, tell me where to turn, tell me where to go;
how you know the heart of a people locked
down in that slave century, how you know
the songs to sing like that? My heart
feels lighter now, tells me that we showed
you something and you doing your part
like we all did; and we still here
still standing, still holding on right here.

III

for Jack Johnson

Forgive me for not moving beyond the well
where they must have found him by the stench
of his body or the flies' cacophonic spell
of alarm — how they found the sour bitch wedged
between the mossy walls, his neck broken,
his busted head black with dried blood;
when they came, a blanket of flies rising
reluctantly to fill the sky. He did not know God,
did not know what breeze off the tracks
could remember all his sins, the brothers
he slaughtered, the women he smacked
about before taking his sick pleasures.
Forgive me for the sweet hymn in my throat.
We who captained the boat will go down with the boat.

IV

for W.E.B. DuBois

That's what the niggers don't realize. If I got one
thing against the black chappies it's this. No one gives
it to you. You have to *take* it.

FRANK COSTELLO (JACK NICHOLSON),
THE DEPARTED

He puts the question well, tradition
or progress? The spirits in the piano
sold for a plot of land, a piece of a nation
so intent on burying us with sorrows,
sell the bloodied past for the hope
of a tomorrow; as if memory and spirit
can be lost, as if we could all cope
with the absence of history. He tells it
well, the conundrum, but is soft
on the answers. Still a sweet entertainment,
this crowding of the poor and bereft,
so much is said in a laborer's pronouncement.
But it is not enough for a future,
if we are to thrive and endure.

V

for Paul Laurence Dunbar

The preacher man counts his coins each day.
In the city you can pretend a heroic past;
a patriot, high in rank, slaughtering the gray-
coated Confederates, a glorious cast
of relatives and friends — you can invent
dreams, riding up and down the elevator,
ferrying white folks who sometimes vent
about stocks and the changing weather,
like you know something, and if you're lucky
they will let you say a poem or two;
a way to make a living to beat back memory
that will snare your feet, consume you.
I like the preacher, I know him well,
caged bird riding between heaven and hell.

VI

for Zora Neale Hurston

Thank God they letting you sing and dance,
talk your vernacular, spin your potions,
and the women take and throw to chance
the men they want and speak what notion
come to their head. Thank the Lord
the negro can be a negro, all alone
on the stage. Welcome, welcome aboard,
I have been waiting for so long.
And now everybody's doing it. Maybe
I feel a little cheated, but I've had
my little spell with glory,
so I will settle myself and not say a bad
word about how ordinary our heroes are
or how to get here we must have traveled far.

Avoiding the Spirits

Berniece: I don't play that piano 'cause I don't want
to wake them spirits. They never be walking around
in this house.

AUGUST WILSON

When at sunset the congregation gathers
in the low light of Saint Helena's old gray
Baptist chapel, they guard their hearts
from the whisper of the low-bellied trees,
calling on the blood as they brush off
the dew on their coats by the burial ground.
When they sing, the sound has the flat
simplicity of prayer, a sound that brings
heat to your neck, tears to your eyes
because you can hear in the rugged
rafters hewed from old-growth trees
at the water's edge, the voices of all those
people who had nothing but lament
and Jesus to fill the gap of a stolen life.
The sisters can't make a man cross
that threshold unless he has come
to lay someone to rest or to witness
a child's blessing or a daughter's
wedding, for a man can't hear the flat
voices in the church and not feel
the droop of his shoulders
and the weight of his dangling
empty hands that have too often
hung helpless for prudence's sake, for good
sense, making him not a man
but an empty shell, a creature
who laughs to stop the shame
of not being able to keep his family

together and safe. No, he would rather
sit in the dark cathedral of the juke
joint and let the blues of sardonic
regret and caustic distance
wash him, make him know that
he is alone on the road, and all
he's got is his story. My people
long gave up on the ancestors
when they learned that those
stepping out of the woods
are the crippled gods, the beaten
gods, the blackened and burned-out
tongueless gods, the broken
gods, the castrated gods, the shadow
gods with questions, asking
us if they will ever heal, asking
for a balm from the living. Who wants
to pour libation for the burdened
spirits? Silence is our salvation,
that and the reassurance of this earth,
this clear air, this forgetting.

The Burden

So sometimes you just want to shoot the poet
because he carries no piano, no guitar,
no horn you could smash or sink
in deep water; the poet is just a head
of conundrums; and you know that
this divining music man, this trickster
with two faces—one to ritualize
holiness, the other to sniff out
the perfume and money in a woman's
skin—this filthy priest with clean
eyes and stained hands is the shadow
you carry for months while these
spirits swirl around you. Young
man, you will die young once
you have exorcised this century
of souls, cast them out into light,
into the bodies of the penitents,
the broken hearts of actors who
give of themselves each night.
Young man, you have always
had an old soul, an ancient
poet's soul, and your back has
carried every instrument of praise
there is, a sack of noises
dragging you down, while you
walk through this world, and
sometimes your forget yourself
because this poet consumes you,
and you wonder who is talking,
who is carrying you down, and you
want to shoot the poet; but
this is all you have left,

quick-stepping dance man,
this is all that makes you breathe,
this journeyman of many voices,
who sometimes, after eating
his fill of the world, will stretch
out and sleep, leaving you
light for a spell, easy in your skin,
finding the calm of death.

Death

First your dog dies and you pray
for the Holy Spirit to raise the inept
lump in the sack, but Jesus's name
is no magic charm; sunsets and the
flies are gathering. That is how faith
dies. By dawn you know death,
the way it arrives and then grows
silent. Death wins. So you walk
out to the tangle of thorny weeds behind
the barn, and you coax a black
cat to your fingers. You let it lick
milk and spit from your hand before
you squeeze its neck until it messes
itself, its claws tearing your skin,
its eyes growing into saucers.
A dead cat is light as a live
one and not stiff, not yet. You
grab its tail and fling it as
far as you can. The crows find
it first; by then the stench
of the hog pens hides the canker
of death. Now you know the power
of death, that you have it,
that you can take life in a second
and wake the same the next day.
This is why you can't fear death.
You have seen the broken neck
of a man in a well, you know who
pushed him over the lip of the well,
tumbling down; you know all about
blood on the ground. You know that
a dead dog is a dead cat is a dead

man. Now you look a white man
in the face, talk to him about
cotton prices and the cost of land,
laugh your wide openmouthed laugh
in his face, and he knows one thing
about you: that you know the power
of death, and you will die as easily
as live. This is how a man seizes
what he wants, how a man
turns the world over in dreams,
eats a solid meal and waits
for death to come like nothing,
like the open sky, like light
at early morning. Like a man
in red pinstriped trousers, a black
top hat, a yellow scarf,
and a kerchief dipped in eau
de cologne to cut through
the stench coming from his mouth.

Fire

He is the man with the ax with its white edge.
He was born to a time of fire.
He took a pickax and walked to the rail
track and asked for work; and he stood
by the sparks and forging fire, standing
there as if the heat were food, pure food.
He is the forger of plans and the man
who has vowed to be a friend
of fire, vowed to teach all flame
the democracy of heat. He was
born to a time of fire, a man
born to turn broken engines
into piston and grease, a man who sees
the world as a machine; everything
will atrophy, all fires must die,
but while the bellows blow. Here is
an ordinary man, big hands, big
dreams, moving through the earth.
A stranger always, a sojourner.
Trains thunder through the green
world, a farm stretches away
from him; to cross from one end
of the country to the other is
the journey from fence to fence,
the grand expanse of someone else's
land that he knows like it is his.
Above, the crackle of a low-flying
plane, and in the river, the clunking
of a steamboat — this is progress,
this is the machine, and a black
man stands on the edge of the monstrosity
of iron and knows he must

be a forge where all heat will channel
energy. Where a body can move,
break ground, fill hands, where
a man can be at the top, commanding
the elements; these are the days
of fire, the days of charred bodies
dangling from trees, the days
of burned-out towns, negroes running
to find their way in the belly
of cities; these are the days
when fire must meet fire.
He was born to a time of fire,
let him burn, baby, let him burn.

Land

Beaufort County, South Carolina

Heading east toward the coast, the air
thickens; the fecund earth yields old growth,
bearded oaks; on the flat highway
the world of encroaching green closes in
on you — then the relay of bridges over
the shallow brackish waters dotted
with colonies of soldier crabs boring
in and out of mud and seagrass;
somewhere on the other side of the bridge
you know you are a stranger, this
land is older than your arrival, it is
older than the aching bodies of new
slaves squatting in circles on the sand,
their bodies covered with sores,
the stipple of shade and light
calming them — some have forgotten
their songs, some their tongues,
and some the idea of tomorrow.
These islands are as old as the crap
and blood planted here, old as
the tough explosion of clapping
hands, old as Jesus in the rafters
of the wooden chapel. A man
would know that he must mark
his passing along the way, that
he must carve out his name
on the trunks of trees, that he
must mark the four corners of his home
with the judicious spill of piss;
a man knows to mark these rice fields,
these cotton fields, these creeks as if
they are his own; it is how he will

journey from the bottom to the top:
each dawn, walking the expanse
of white people's land, marking trees,
pissing, pissing, before sinking
hoe into soil, before bleeding into
soil, before spitting into soil.
This is how you understand
the ancestry of land; and you,
interloper, Johnny-come-lately,
you must learn the rituals
of centuries of folks claiming what
was not their own, centuries
of folks turning the earth into the basic
trace of memory, the purchase of a dream.

To Tame the Savage Beast

You learn the chemistry of linseed,
the softening of beeswax; the muscles
you grow in your forearm make
you able to break the tiny bones
in a white child's hands, you have
thought of this. You watch her
float along the blackened boards,
her feet bruised red with fever,
as she settles at the piano, her white
bundle of fabric swelling about
her. She looks at you to see
if you have paused to hear;
and as always, she mutters,
"Taming the heart of the beast"—
She looks at you with a soft
smile as she does to her
cats or the idiot dog she feeds
to bloated grogginess. You
look back, smile a smile
of stones before she begins to
play. All these years, you have
heard the sound as the anthem
of blood, broken glass, smashed wood,
clicking bones sliced by a heavy
cutlass, the choking squeal
of breathlessness, the grunt
before silence — all these years,
your eyes have rested on the faces
of your blood, carved by your father's
steady hand into the piano; soft
wood; this crowd of holy witness
she relishes, pitifully spoiled

bitch who just wanted to keep
her brown-faced negroes around her.
You come closer, place your hands
on the embossment of bodies,
a shape you have caressed
with oil for years, a shape
you whisper to at night, a shape
that, come the grand finale,
walks out of the wood, stands
sentinel around the piano and this
white woman, and issues
a riot of laughter and shame
over her. You will soon slip
away, knowing that it is not yet
time, your arms twitching,
your fists clasping and unclasping.

Mama

I

Before the squat bungalows of rough-hewn
timber felled with two-manned saws
at the edge of the river, everything is new:
the silence of the sky, the soft caw
of crows; and we are landed on pebbles,
strangers a long way from home, the sound
of a language climbing in terrible
error through our heads, spinning around,
searching for an echo or a familiar
tongue to speak it. I came before
these cluttered huts where a village,
before the relief of arrival, was the only cure
for the fear; before they saw us niggers
as anything but company, as fellow travelers.

II

First thing you do is walk out in the bush
before dawn, stand in the deep and breathe;
you have to smell to know how to crush
leaf after leaf, to smell out grief
and joy, healing and curses. Everything
is strange, and yet, if you taste the air
everything becomes familiar as breathing,
familiar as the taste of river water,
and you wait for the spirits to talk,
and if they talk funny, they will teach
you their language — show you where to walk,
what twigs to pick up, what leaves
to soak. They know your anointing,
and this is why they keep on giving.

III

News comes in whispers, an exchange of tales
between a simple valet and a field hand,
just where the sweating horses sip from a pail
of cool water; it carries over roads, angry bands of slaves
      returning to their dark cottages.
It can take weeks, months sometimes, but
it comes — so many dead, so many savaged
by white folks, so scared of how close the rot
of brutality came to destroying them. "Stono,"
they whisper, Angolan slaves rising up,
and they shed blood, watched its slow
spill into the earth; they burned down crops,
these, our sustenance, now our ancestors
flying east, far east, sailing homeward.

IV

For every elegant face molded into peace,
every stiff eye kneaded shut, for every bath
in mint, cinnamon, ginger, and warmed aloes,
you understand the languages spoken on this path
through thickening bush; for each body
laid out on wood, orifices washed, fingers cleaned,
you fear nothing of their secret mysteries
of flesh and blood, broken bread and wine.
We plant broken bottles and shells in the ground
then wait for the returning sun to promise
a safe passage; and you swell with song,
full of the holy food that nourishes
you — you grow fat after each burial,
as silent as history, stoic, regal.

V

All around the trees' leaves are black
with burn and dry blood. The stench
of flesh will continue to attack
our dreams. I learn to know pink
skin, though black with rot, from
the pulping of my brothers' bodies.
My job is to search out from the worms
something to keep, to undo the mystery
of the dead—nothing new in this.
We must haul the tender limbs
onto wagons, then bury them. Ah hubris,
look at what our arrogance brings!
This war, too, will pass, but I
will not forget the fresh scent of a kill.

VI

Deep in August, news comes in starts,
six hundred souls perished in Mobile;
a wicked wind turned its eye to blast
into the soft belly of the first hills
rising out of the gulf, and negroes
have been walking aimlessly for weeks.
The heat is cooking everything; mosquitoes
taking the babies home. It's bleak,
the future — I will leave these dried-out
fields for the dip and rise of green
valleys. Pittsburgh with its tugboats
plying the crisscrossing of rivers, the scream
of steel factory whistles, the stroke of hope
in the sky: soon we'll all learn to cope.

Exorcism

for Edgar Allan Poe

The drunk see into the gloom, hear voices:
the drunk bluesman knows the mist
of unsettled spirits, he shouts loudly
at the way his skin pimples as if
a soft cold wind had stirred in this oven
of a Pittsburgh tenement; the dead
are drawn to the promise of whiskey.

How casual he is after sweaty
wrestling with the beast; how calmly
he walks away after — as if he has
done this before, the dance of bodies
hurled against walls — it is not
easy to kill a man with your hands:
they will fight with everything to live.

Any child who sees the bloated
body of a familiar spirit, even once,
will be marked for life — not a curse
but a queer anointing, as if
the dead are always with us. She
knows that you can wrestle
the dead, silence them with a body
alert to its every muscle; she learns.

"The Old Ship of Zion" fills the room.
So many ships have held the unsettled
dreams of black folk. Now the "Old Ship
of Zion" stirs some ancient gene
that makes the glinting
ripple of open water trigger

for tears, for memories older than
reason. "The Old Ship of Zion" rocks
against the nudge of waves,
and the fear of death by drowning
returns to the women who sing
in that robust voice while the spirit
stares through the gloom.

The drunk man will collapse
eventually, all fight gone.
The fighter's body will give way,
the neck's strain, the taut
press against all peace.
This child will see and know.
Sing, woman; sing, woman, sing!

Old Man under a Pecan Tree

Two trucks and five dogs behind the chain-link;
you come up to this pecan-tree-shaded
colonial ranch bungalow, squatting low
and brown in the deep green. A man sits
as always, under the crowd of shadow
and light, looking over the low fence
to the stretch of tobacco and soy, acres spread
out under the constant Southern sky—from
here, the rumble of the freight and the
midnight howl of the clandestine Amtrak
takes him into the history, long before
stocks and shares, government subsidies,
401(k)s, the gleaming monstrous trucks panting
in the driveway. Ask him about life,
he will tell you about the great-grands
living up in Pittsburgh or the favorite
girl running things in the legislature —
how far we have come, what a truck-
load of watermelons and the ingenuity
of two felons can do. He has bad dreams
of France, the blasted bodies of soldiers,
the mud, the idle hours waiting for
bombs, the dead, the dry dead on green
fields, staring; those are his only nightmares.
The rest are battle trophies: the funerals
for those big-bellied white landowners,
all dead falling into wells—a breeze,
a circle of confusion from whiskeys
on a suffocating August day, a wrong
step, a flood of guilt for a life of sin
sending them hurtling their useless selves
into the mossy wells — all trophies, the things

a man can look at and say, "God is watching."
He is a man at peace with it all, when
you find him, when you come off the two-
lane highway, right by Talbot's
peach stand and liquor store, take the old
dust road for four miles in until you come
to a long stand of pecan trees, and this
homestead of cool air, dogs, and rusting
trucks — you will find him here — he never
left. They all went, headed North,
got a new language, but he came back,
even after the war, after white women,
after good wine, he came back, old country
boy, to keep the gravestones washed clean,
to stand guard, to sometimes walk
to that place where the tracks used
to cross, to squat on the stony ground
and listen to the ghosts of those boys
thanking him for staying back to hear
them. He knows he has the power
to keep those spirits where they must
stay: and when he goes, he will
have a hand on them, and that
would be good, so good.

The Lessons

Fingers can be trained to make shapes
that, pressed just right on the gleaming
keys, will make a sound that can stay
tears or cause them to flow for days.
Anyone can learn to make some music,
but not all have the heart to beat
out the tunes that will turn us inside out.

Knowing how to play this thing is a gift
and a curse. Left alone in the bone
all our demons will come and occupy
the dry warm places we have left
wide open for the cultivators of despair,
and discord, to fill. The silence
is not a voice but an absence
as weighty as the heavy air in fog.

Everything, the new-century man
says, has a price. The art is in
the alchemy of turning trash to cash.
It is longing that will make us
give what we must hear, and sound
that will wash us with the sweet
hollow feeling that comes after tears.
Somebody will pay for this
every time. This is another lesson.

That woman's barrenness is a dress
she wears each morning. Her
body still remembers the supple
swoop of her thighs moving to desire,
but this dress will dry out even

the pliant give of music she has
made for years. She is beating
back laughter with lament and anger;
and the drought devours the open field.

Things carry the blood and bone
of their makers. A careful listener
will hear the sigh and grunt of labor
in the gleaming wood of the piano.
Those faces, those bodies are etched
into the face of the cherrywood
and the music knocking its way
out through the pores is the blood.
Left silent, a dryness takes hold,
a dull crumbling rot sets in.

The ghosts make deals with the air.
After a while an unwelcome room
will empty of the unwelcome.
Remember this always: a full
woman, straight-backed, playing
the piano with her breath held
so deep in her it moves her hips,
and when her voice fills the room
the unwelcome flees, just like that.

Index of First Lines

Index of Titles

About the Author

Kwame Dawes is currently the Glenna Luschei Editor-in-Chief of *Prairie Schooner* at the University of Nebraska–Lincoln, where he is a Chancellor's Professor of English, a faculty member of Cave Canem, and a teacher in the Pacific MFA program in Oregon. He is cofounder and programming director of the biennial Calabash International Literary Festival, which takes place in Jamaica. He is a regular blogger for the Poetry Foundation; his blogs can be read at www. poetryfoundation.org.

About the Editor

Matthew Shenoda is the author of the poetry collections *Seasons of Lotus, Seasons of Bone* and *Somewhere Else,* winner of the American Book Award. He is currently Associate Professor and Associate Dean of the School of Fine and Performing Arts at Columbia College Chicago. For more information visit: www.matthewshenoda.com.

Poetry is vital to language and living. Since 1972, Copper
Canyon Press has published extraordinary poetry from
around the world to engage the imaginations and intellects
of readers, writers, booksellers, librarians, teachers, students,
and donors.

WE ARE GRATEFUL FOR THE MAJOR SUPPORT PROVIDED BY:

THE PAUL G. ALLEN
FAMILY FOUNDATION

THE MAURER FAMILY
FOUNDATION

NATIONAL
ENDOWMENT
FOR THE ARTS

WASHINGTON STATE
ARTS COMMISSION

Anonymous

Arcadia Fund

John Branch

Diana and Jay Broze

Beroz Ferrell & The Point, LLC

Mimi Gardner Gates

Gull Industries, Inc.
on behalf of William and Ruth True

Mark Hamilton and Suzie Rapp

Carolyn and Robert Hedin

Steven Myron Holl

Rhoady and Jeanne Marie Lee

Maureen Lee and Mark Busto

New Mexico Community Foundation

H. Stewart Parker

Penny and Jerry Peabody

Joseph C. Roberts

Cynthia Lovelace Sears and Frank Buxton

The Seattle Foundation

Charles and Barbara Wright

The dedicated interns and faithful
volunteers of Copper Canyon Press

To learn more about underwriting Copper Canyon Press titles,
please call 360-385-4925 ext. 103

The Chinese character for poetry is made up of two parts: "word" and "temple." It also serves as pressmark for Copper Canyon Press.

The interior is set in Miller, a "Scotch Roman" designed by Matthew Carter in 1997. The display type is set in Interstate, designed by Tobias Frere-Jones. Book design by VJBScribe. Printed on archival-quality paper at McNaughton & Gunn, Inc.